ADVANCE PRAISE FOR

Radical Animal Studies: Beyond Respectability Politics, Opportunism, and Cooptation

"In recent years, the importance of social movements has become more of an important part of advancing critical animal studies toward what Socha and Nocella propose as radical animal studies. *Radical Animal Studies: Beyond Respectability Politics, Opportunism, and Cooptation* offers a timely collection of thoughtful essays that center diversity in activist-scholarship and teach of the importance of radical theory and action through (and with) social movements that include animal liberation together with social justice."
—Johnny Lupinacci, Associate Professor, Cultural Studies and Social Thought in Education, Washington State University

"This timely book offers up important insights, distinctions, and analyses for the theory and practice for animal liberation, but also for social movements in general. Anyone serious about radical social change should read and discuss this book. It will improve your push for a better world!"
—Jason Del Gandio, Author, *Rhetoric for Radicals: A Handbook for 21st Century Activists*

"This important book affords animal liberation scholars and activists an opportunity to move beyond traditional liberal conceptions of animal rights theory and practice. Readers will learn how 'radical' and 'radicalism' are not dirty words, but rather essential means through which to achieve the total liberation of species. It should be considered an essential reading in critical animal studies."
—S. Marek Muller, Florida Atlantic University; Author, *Impersonating Animals: Rhetoric, Ecofeminism, and Animal Rights Law*

Radical Animal Studies

RADICAL ANIMAL STUDIES AND TOTAL LIBERATION

Anthony J. Nocella II
Series Editor

Vol. 8

The Radical Animal Studies and Total Liberation series
is part of the Peter Lang Education list.
Every volume is peer reviewed and meets
the highest quality standards for content and production.

PETER LANG
New York • Bern • Berlin
Brussels • Vienna • Oxford • Warsaw

Radical Animal Studies

Beyond Respectability Politics,
Opportunism, and Cooptation

Edited by
Anthony J. Nocella II
and Kim Socha

PETER LANG
New York • Bern • Berlin
Brussels • Vienna • Oxford • Warsaw

Library of Congress Cataloging-in-Publication Data

Names: Nocella, Anthony J., editor. | Socha, Kim, editor.
Title: Radical animal studies: beyond respectability politics,
opportunism, and cooptation / edited by Anthony J. Nocella II and Kim Socha.
Description: New York: Peter Lang, 2022.
Series: Radical animal studies and total liberation; vol. 8
ISSN 2469-3065 (print) | ISSN 2469-3081 (online)
Includes bibliographical references and index.
Identifiers: LCCN 2021033836 (print) | LCCN 2021033837 (ebook)
ISBN 978-1-4331-9156-5 (hardback) | ISBN 978-1-4331-9157-2 (paperback)
ISBN 978-1-4331-9158-9 (ebook pdf) | ISBN 978-1-4331-9159-6 (epub)
Subjects: LCSH: Animal rights—Political aspects. | Animal
welfare—Political aspects. | Animal rights activists. | Radicalism.
Classification: LCC HV4708 .R295 2021 (print) | LCC HV4708 (ebook) |
DDC 636.08/32—dc23
LC record available at https://lccn.loc.gov/2021033836
LC ebook record available at https://lccn.loc.gov/2021033837
DOI 10.3726/b18808

Bibliographic information published by **Die Deutsche Nationalbibliothek**.
Die Deutsche Nationalbibliothek lists this publication in the "Deutsche
Nationalbibliografie"; detailed bibliographic data are available
on the Internet at http://dnb.d-nb.de/.

To Tim Phillips – in the aftermath of rebellious acts, he is a true radical who helps others navigate a system that can be criminal in its failure to mete out justice.

Table of Contents

Acknowledgements

We would like to thank the publisher Peter Lang Publishing, contributors—David Pellow, Will Boisseau, Erika Cudworth, Richard J. White, Kyle Ramsey-Sumner and Piper Ramsey-Sumner, Jess Ison, and Michael Loadenthal, and those that wrote blurbs for the book—Dr. Johnny Lupinacci, Dr. Jason Del Gandio, S. Marek Muller, Lucas Alan, Jason Bayless, Alisha Page, Marisol Burgueno, and Arash Daneshzadeh. We would love to thank our many organizations we are involved with such as—Institute for Critical Animal Studies, Academy for Peace Education, Utah Reintegration Project, Save the Kids, Wisdom Behind the Walls, Peace Studies Journal, Transformative Justice Journal, Arissa Media Group, Salt Lake Peace and Justice, Poetry Behind the Walls, Eco-Ability Collective, and Utah Alternatives to Violence Project. We most importantly like to thank our friends and family whose love is essential to our being.

Foreword
Burn, Baby(lon), Burn

David Naguib Pellow

In November 1997, activists with the Animal Liberation Front (ALF) and the Earth Liberation Front (ELF) undertook a joint action involving arson at a Bureau of Land Management (BLM) horse corral near Burns, Oregon. Before burning the facility to the ground, the activists released more than five hundred wild horses and burros into the wild. The joint public statement read, in part:

> The Bureau of Land Management (BLM) claims they are removing non-native species from public lands (aren't white Europeans also non-native) but then they turn around and subsidize the cattle industry and place thousands of non-native domestic cattle on these same lands. . . . [This action was taken] to help halt the BLM's illegal and immoral business of rounding up wild horses from public lands and funneling them to slaughter. This hypocrisy and genocide against the horse nation will not go unchallenged!"– Animal Liberation Front, Earth Liberation Front.

At a recent national animal rights conference, an activist who had served prison time for his role in releasing thousands of minks from fur farms in the midwestern U.S., discussed the merits of arson in animal liberation: "The first ALF arson action in 1987 was at UC Davis, in the Animal Diagnostic Building. That cost them $4 million. Since then, we've seen 106 arsons by ALF. Arson can be very effective. It's fire, it gets the job done. It's fast and requires minimal people."

In November 2007, animal liberation activist Jonathan Paul pled guilty to one count of conspiracy and one count of arson for his role in the 1997 burning of the Cavel West horsemeat slaughterhouse in Redmond, Oregon, which destroyed the plant and led to its permanent closure. Even though no one was injured in the fire, federal prosecutors described it as a "classic case of terrorism." Paul was arrested as part of the FBI's 2005 Operation Backfire. He began serving a fifty-one-month sentence at FCI Phoenix in October 2007.

The kind of activism that animal liberationists like ALF members have engaged in for many years often gets labeled as "violence." But property destruction—particularly the destruction of property that has been used in the service of killing on an industrial scale—pales by comparison to the mass atrocities perpetrated by corporations and states against non-human species on a daily basis. There simply is no comparison and certainly no equivalence, particularly when one act is aimed at *preventing* further harm while the other is part of a casual, largely unquestioned sequence of otherwise unending and unnecessary pain and suffering.

Radical Animal Studies is a book that is sorely needed in this age of mass violence and mass distraction from that violence. This collection of authors, activist-scholars, and revolutionaries is refreshing in its brazen defense of free-dom from all forms of oppression, by any means necessary. This group of radical intellectuals and visionaries speaks powerful and empowering truths by setting aside the pretensions and the cold "objectivity" of the neolib-eral academy and saying out loud (and in broad daylight) that they insist on and expect nothing less than total liberation from all systems of domination. *Radical Animal Studies* (as a book and a new field of inquiry and action) is also a breath of fresh air in that it embraces humor and humility. As the editors note, this book is "not the final word on what it means to engage in RAS" and they invite a wide spectrum of thinkers, activists, anarchists, deviants, and miscreants to join them in joyful revelry and revolution. I am delighted and honored to count myself among this honorable community.

In true guerrilla fashion, like so many revolutionaries before them, ALF activists declared that there would have to be consequences for the unaccept-able practices associated with speciesism, dominionism, ecocide, and massive animal slaughter, although clearly recognizing the reality of power asymme-tries between Empire and the underground resistance. ALF communiqués are a love letter to the Earth and her/their multispecies denizens, and a way of putting Babylon on notice: "if you build it, we will burn it down to the ground." The use of fire as a means of protest, resistance, expression, and revolution has a long and storied history. As an African American and animal liberationist, I write this essay at a time when so many of us are taking to the streets on a regular basis to protest racist police violence in America, activism that is often accompanied by arson directed at local police stations and busi-nesses. My ancestors deployed the tool of arson—burning down the master's house or the sugar cane fields (or both!)—as a means of striking a blow against the slaveocracy upon which the U.S. was founded. This is indeed a time-honored method of practicing politics by other means, and is celebrated in many popular cultural forms. The classic song by the Trammps, "Disco Inferno," features the infamous line "burn, baby burn, burn that mother down." When I was a teenager, one of my favorite songs was "The Roof is On Fire" by the hip-hop artists Rock Master Scott and the Dynamic Three. It became something of an anthem that young people in my community sang gleefully, especially the lines: "The roof, the roof, the roof is on fire. We don't need no water, let the motherf___r burn!" African American comedian Steve Harvey adds humor to this tradition in his sketch about a fictive Black employee facing imminent termination by his boss when he says, "Say I'm fired and I'll set this motherf___ on fire! I'll burn this motherf____ to the ground!" Reggae artist John Holt's swaggering and mutinous song "Police in Helicopter" echoes and prefigures the ALF's warning with the lyrics: "But if you continue to burn up the Herbs, we gonna burn down the cane fields." The use of fire—whether literally or figuratively—is a powerful means of communicating a refusal to cooperate with systems of discrimination and oppression.

Radical Animal Studies offers an inspiring and productive opening for readers who find themselves in search of a compelling rationale for why and how they might persuasively articulate a route toward multi-issue, transformative, and radical thinking and action that links multiple social justice struggles across populations, species, and geographies. Read this book, debate its questions, claims, and arguments with your friends and family, and light a fire inside you in order to blaze your own path toward total liberation.

Preface
Radicals Help Make It Practical

Aaron Zellhoefer

It's not radical. If you are against the abuse of women, you will always speak up and act out, regardless of the consequences. If you are against the abuse of children, you will always speak up and act out, regardless of the consequences. If you are against the abuse of animals, you will always speak up and act out, regardless of the consequences. This is not exactly a verbatim quote, but this is what I interpreted from an early article in *No Compromise*, a radical publication for the animal liberation movement from the mid-1990s to the early 2000s. The point was over the legitimacy of the radical edge in our movement.

Nobody cares about the radical edge in other moments, especially those that advanced their causes. Anne Hansen and the Wimmin's Fire Brigade firebombed a pornography shop that was selling child pornography. The Suffragettes gave their lives, smashed windows, and set fires for the right for women to vote. Harriet Tubman helped free slaves; she worked alongside John Brown to plan the attack on Harpers Ferry. Tubman, Brown, and abolitionist writer Fredrick Douglass were considered radicals of their days, but history showed them on the right side of history because in retrospect, we know they did the right thing.

But when animal activists break property and liberate animals, we are labeled thugs and terrorists. We have done nothing more than help end the suffering of living beings by using tactics that other liberationists have used. The media loves to use the word "radical" to show we are extreme and out of touch with society. They use the word "radical" to undermine our movement. Our job is to show that we are actually speaking for the values of society and on the issues at stake. Our aim is to show that our actions are not radical, but practical. "Radicals" help push a practical agenda which helps eliminate animal suffering.

Radicals bring negative press, but their actions can bring long term success. Case in point: illegal attacks on the fur industry in California. In the 19990s, Neiman Marcus had several attacks on its business in California. I attended a "We Love the ALF" demonstration at Neiman Marcus after the ALF had smashed out multiple display windows at Neiman Marcus' San Francisco store. The press condemned the tactic, but the issue of suffering was brought to the masses. It helped created a shift in opinion which eventually led to a ban of the sale of fur in the state of California in 2019. Radicals, though not necessarily working hand-in- hand with the moderates who took the legal route, helped make this monumental shift.

In regards to animal testing, there had probably been hundreds of attacks on the animal testing industry, either directly or indirectly, in the state of California. Again, the press condemned the tactic, but this helped bring some very graphic footage to the masses and eventually brought about a cosmetic testing ban in California. Radicals, again, helped jump start this issue.

The same happened with foie gras. When activists liberated ducks used in the production of foie gras and caused damage at a restaurant that was going to sell the product, the issue of the force feeding of ducks and geese was brought to the forefront. Within months, there were public hearings on the issue and an attempt to ban the sale was discussed. Ultimately, a ban would go into effect, though the courts would eventually overrule it.

Looking back at history, this dynamic has always been the case. Radicals have helped push the envelope to get the moderates to the table to take on next steps.

In the aftermath of the assassination of Martin Luther King Jr. in April 1968, the Holy Week Uprising took place with riots taking place in over 100 cities. Within a week, the Civil Rights Act of 1968 came into effect.

In the 1970s, the George Jackson Brigade bombed a Safeway supermarket partly to contest the working conditions of the farm workers producing grapes for the store. Caesar Chávez would later work with grape growers to improve the lives of those farm workers.

In current times, we have seen global protests and uprisings in the aftermath of the killing of George Floyd by four police officers on May 25, 2020 in Minneapolis, Minnesota. Their basic message: justice must be served in this latest police killing. Over 700 buildings in Minneapolis were either fully burned to the ground, partially burned, or heavily damaged. Just over a month later, the Minneapolis City Council unanimously voted to dismantle the Police Department. This very radical thought has now become a practical reality.

All in all, radicals would rather have the public mantra of, "I agree with your message and not your tactics," than, "I agree with your tactics, but not your message."

Personally, I have seen what radical politics can do to end oppression. Sometimes radical actions alone can end abuse. This is the case with Hillgrove Cat Farm (cat breeders for vivisection), Shamrock (primate breeders for vivisection), Consort Beagles (beagle breeders for vivisection), Newchurch (guinea pig breeders for vivisection), and Regal Rabbits (rabbit breeders for vivisection). All have closed because of radical, direct action based campaigns against them. In the case of Stop Huntingdon Animal Cruelty (SHAC), we did not directly close down Huntingdon Life Sciences (HLS); however, I don't think the campaign was a complete failure. Radical activists did push the envelope, started conversations and changed the narrative on vivisection.

This brings me to *Radical Animal Studies*, an important book that offers readers an understanding of the word "radical" and an overview of its practical possibilities. Social change makers, no matter where they fall on the spectrum of tactics, must gain an understanding of what it means to be "radical," the historical implications of the term, and the achievements radicals have made in the world.

Introduction: Outside the Realm of Negotiation: From Underground to Battleground

KIM SOCHA AND ANTHONY J. NOCELLA II

Parsing and Principles

In 2006, Critical Animal Studies (CAS) was founded after much verbal and written correspondence among a number of people, including Steve Best, Richard Kahn, John Sorenson, and Anthony J. Nocella II (Nocella, Sorenson, Socha, & Matsuoka, 2013). Despite best intentions for a radical approach to animal liberation in the academy, Anthony surmised that eventually CAS would be coopted by opportunists and careerists within and outside universities and colleges. However, they persevered with CAS, as they knew it would shake up traditional narratives in the short term and, if needed, could eventually move toward Radical Animal Studies (RAS) just as critical pedagogy moved to radical pedagogy and critical criminology to radical criminology.

To understand Critical Animal Studies (CAS), it is helpful to also understand that despite similarities in name, CAS is not Animal Studies (AS) or Human-Animal Studies (HAS). As Waldau (2013) explains, a primary goal of AS is to put nonhuman animals in the "foreground," which is important. However, despite best efforts, humans always seem to become the center of attention, as AS scholars are prompted to "explore humans' possibilities with other animals in personally relevant ways" (p. x). Thus, an AS proponent may use the field to investigate human-animal relations or explore animality in humans. AS may be practiced by a neuroscientist studying primate conduct in captivity or an art historian documenting the changing depiction of wolves and human responses to them in the Western visual arts. In sum, it is not focused on animal liberation in any radical way.

HAS is even more human-focused as "an interdisciplinary field that explores the spaces that animals occupy in human social and cultural worlds and the interactions humans have with them. Central to this field is an exploration of the ways in which animal lives intersect with human societies" (DeMello, 2013, p. 4). An HAS student, therefore, can look forward to careers in zoos, veterinary medicine, and laboratory sciences. Unlike AS, there is nothing liberatory about HAS. In fact, as a field, it is part of the problem that CAS has sought to remedy: the view that non-humans are a means to human ends.

In stark contrast, CAS adheres to ten principles that all proponents of it were, and still are, expected to support and respect. At the very least, scholars and activists should build off of this foundation and actively work not to contradict the principles. In 2007, Best, Nocella, Kahn, Carol Gigliotti, and Lisa Kemmerer, developed "The Ten Principles of Critical Animal Studies," which follow here:

1. Pursues interdisciplinary collaborative writing and research in a rich and comprehensive manner that includes perspectives typically ignored by animal studies such as political economy.
2. Rejects pseudo-objective academic analysis by explicitly clarifying its normative values and political commitments, such that there are no positivist illusions whatsoever that theory is disinterested or writing and research is nonpolitical. To support experiential understanding and subjectivity.
3. Eschews narrow academic viewpoints and the debilitating theory-for-theory's sake position in order to link theory to practice, analysis to politics, and the academy to the community.
4. Advances a holistic understanding of the commonality of oppressions, such that speciesism, sexism, racism, ableism, statism, classism, militarism and other hierarchical ideologies and institutions are viewed as parts of a larger, interlocking, global system of domination.
5. Rejects apolitical, conservative, and liberal positions in order to advance an anti-capitalist, and, more generally, a radical anti-hierarchical politics. This orientation seeks to dismantle all structures of exploitation, domination, oppression, torture, killing, and power in favor of decentralizing and democratizing society at all levels and on a global basis.
6. Rejects reformist, single-issue, nation-based, legislative, strictly animal interest politics in favor of alliance politics and solidarity with other struggles against oppression and hierarchy.

7. Champions a politics of total liberation which grasps the need for, and the inseparability of, human, nonhuman animal, and Earth liberation and freedom for all in one comprehensive, though diverse, struggle; to quote Martin Luther King Jr.: "Injustice anywhere is a threat to justice everywhere."

8. Deconstructs and reconstructs the socially constructed binary oppositions between human and nonhuman animals, a move basic to mainstream animal studies, but also looks to illuminate related dichotomies between culture and nature, civilization and wilderness and other dominator hierarchies to emphasize the historical limits placed upon humanity, nonhuman animals, cultural/political norms, and the liberation of nature as part of a transformative project that seeks to transcend these limits towards greater freedom, peace, and ecological harmony.

9. Openly supports and examines controversial radical politics and strategies used in all kinds of social justice movements, such as those that involve economic sabotage from boycotts to direct action toward the goal of peace.

10. Seeks to create openings for constructive critical dialog on issues relevant to Critical Animal Studies across a wide-range of academic groups; citizens and grass roots activists; the staffs of policy and social service organizations; and people in private, public, and non-profit sectors. Through – and only through – new paradigms of ecopedagogy, bridge-building with other social movements, and a solidarity-based alliance politics, it is possible to build the new forms of consciousness, knowledge, and social institutions that are necessary to dissolve the hierarchical society that has enslaved this planet for the last ten thousand years (pp. 4–5).

CAS scholars do not necessarily focus on all ten principles in their activism and research. They might only be concerned with two or three principles. Of course, they are not actively opposed to any of the principles. This brings us to the importance of Radical Animal Studies (RAS), a subfield of CAS. RAS is focused on total liberation and underground movements such as the Animal Liberation Front (ALF) and the Earth Liberation Front (ELF) (Best & Nocella, 2004; Best & Nocella, 2006). RAS is most concerned with Principle 7 (total liberation) and Principle 9 (revolutionary groups, specifically the ALF). The purpose of RAS, therefore, is to study the history of the animal advocacy movement while also examining social movement tactics and strategies most fit towards the goals of animal liberation and total liberation. To fully grasp the import of the ninth principle, proponents of RAS should know their history, if only a bit for starters.

A Bit of History

In 1974, Ronnie Lee and Cliff Goodman, two long-time animal rights activists, were arrested at Oxford Laboratory in Bicester and sentenced to prison. Their actions against the laboratory included liberating animals, destroying property, and documenting the exploitation of nonhuman animals. Their case garnered mass media coverage which was sympathetic both to their efforts to save nonhuman animals from torture and death and to Lee's prison hunger strike, which was intended to publicize the government's biological and chemical warfare experiments on nonhuman animals. Paroled after a year, Lee renewed his efforts to save animals by creating the ALF in 1976. In contrast to this noble project, Cliff Goodman snitched on Lee for the illegal actions he was accused of.

By 2005, the ALF had active cells all over the world, and the Federal Bureau of Investigations (FBI) had labeled it a top domestic terrorist threat as an act of political repression (Gandio & Nocella, 2014). Unsure what to make of the de-centralized ALF, the FBI designated it as an organization, though it isn't one in the formal sense of the term, as anyone can become an ALF actor without sanction from an organizing body. Rather, the ALF can be seen as a concept to spur on liberatory action for animals based on the following principles:

1. To inflict economic damage on those who profit from the misery and exploitation of animals.
2. To liberate animals from places of abuse, i.e. laboratories, factory farms, fur farms etc., and place them in good homes where they may live out their natural lives, free from suffering.
3. To reveal the horror and atrocities committed against animals behind locked doors, by performing nonviolent direct actions and liberations.
4. To take all necessary precautions against harming any animal, human and nonhuman (as cited in Best & Nocella, 2004, p. 8)

These guidelines have remained unedited since 1976 when the ALF was founded. Ironically, the principles of this non-organization with no employees, no grants, no funding, no offices, no faces, and no leaders have encapsulated at least one goal, or more, of most mainstream organizations in the modern animal rights movement, even those organizations that would attempt to distance themselves from the ALF for public appeal purposes while secretly applauding their efforts.

Every animal rights organization addresses at least one of the four guidelines. The problem is that many activists in the animal advocacy movement today do not know of the ALF or the history of the animal advocacy movement in general, thereby missing the opportunity to learn from the past and adopt or adapt from the wheel of successful (and not-so-successful) social movement tactics and strategies.

Popular organizations such as Anonymous for the Voiceless, Mercy for Animals, and Direct Action Everywhere use tactics of the ALF: filming and photographing animal exploitation, showing such footage to the public, rescuing nonhuman animals, using the media to promote these actions, etc. Other organizations such as People for the Ethical Treatment of Animals, In Defense of Animals, and Last Chance for Animals hold up graphic posters at protests that would not exist if not for the footage of animal abuse covertly taken first by the ALF and then by others who risk their freedom and mental wellbeing to enter places of animal torture to document what's inside.

The Purpose of RAS

So what? You might ask. Is RAS's sole purpose to get modern animal liberation groups to acknowledge their elders and admit to their lack of originality? No. (Such a stance smacks of an intellectual property rights gibe coming from those who are supposed to despise private property rights and advocate peace, harmony, and unity. Right?) Rather, RAS maintains the idea that animal liberation can happen – *can only happen* – as a radical movement, not solely as a rights one, a welfare one, nor progressive one, and not as one that is detached from other liberatory movements for parity. RAS maintains that you cannot differentiate animal liberation from issues of class, gender, citizenship, ability, sexuality, race, culture, or geography (Nocella, White, & Cudworth, 2015). RAS understands that all social movements and struggles are entangled. CAS is grounded in anarchism, thus RAS, as a subfield of CAS, is also grounded in anarchism, which is opposed to authoritarianism, domination, oppression, and exploitation (Amster, DeLeon, Fernandez, Nocella, & Shannon, 2009).

The error in ignoring a movement's history isn't just a petty "acknowledge the past" plea; rather, only by acknowledging the past can you see that your actions for animals have a radical foundation, and any attempts to ignore that foundation and mollify it for the mainstream are bound to fail because true animal liberation is a radical idea. Mainstreaming it leads to vegan Whoppers™ but not and never to the concept that nonhuman animals' lives mean anything of true import. Many activists start out with one primary movement that draws them into the radical sphere. From there, they come to learn of fellow social movements and determine that while the experience of oppression is different, the oppressor is the same (Nocella & George, 2019). *That oppressor is the material manifestation of a mindset that sees living beings as things to be exploited and elements of nature as things to be bought and sold* (Freire, 1997). If you're against that, you have a strong foundation upon which to build alliances with a variety of social movements.

From a theoretical perspective, RAS is here to provide research on and educate others about the importance of underground resistance and revolutionary history to shaping the next phase of animal liberation activism (Nocella, Parson, George, & Eccles, 2019). From a practical perspective, it is here because the animal underground has reached the surface as it never has before in history, and that gauntlet is in the hands of activists who don't know their movement is radical and who would, perhaps, shun the very idea for fear of looking like weirdos to those who abuse animal for profit and pleasure.

Outline of Book

All of the author-activists in this book ascribe to the principles of CAS, and thus of RAS, but while you'll find a smattering of CAS principles peppered within their words, each author can be generally categorized as exploring either Principle 7 (total liberation) or Principle 9 (revolutionary history and/ or current strategy).

With a focus in Principle 9, the first chapter by Kim Socha, "Make-Believe Revolutions Make Make-Believe Revolutionaries" focuses on the promise and pitfalls of being inspired by revolutionary action without clear strategies and goals in place. Sometimes, charging in full-steam pays dividends; other times, it doesn't, as her chapter demonstrates. Moving to Principle 7, Will Boisseau explores where the animal liberation movement fits (and doesn't) within the broader spectrum of leftist movements in "Listening to and Learning from Leftist Critiques of Animal Liberation." RAS encourages animal activists to form alliances with other movements. This chapter offers some answers to the questions, "But do they even want us there, and if not, why not?" Returning to Principle 9 in "Bringing Down the Animal Abuse Industry by Any Means Necessary," Erika Cudworth and Richard White analyze how the revolution might be televised through humor. This introduction to "laughtivism" offers novel ways of using mockery and satire to confront animal cruelty. Next, in "Radicalizing Animal Theology: Moving toward a Revolutionary Praxis,"

Kyle and Piper Ramsey-Sumner stick with Principle 9 by exploring the role of religion in fomenting a revolution for animals, as most theologians sensitive to the plight of animals have mirrored conventional organizations in their approach. In response, the Ramsey-Sumners offer a model of radical religious resistance. Finally, Michael Loadenthal's "Days of War, Knights of Tempeh," is equal parts 7 and 9 as he connects animal liberation to the anti-capitalist, anti-racist, pro-queer anarchist motto that "none are free until all are free" through a catalog of global actions for animals that coexist under the aegis of "total liberation."

The work we offer you in *Radical Animal Studies: Beyond Respectability Politics, Opportunism, and Cooptation* is not the final word on what it means to engage in RAS. It is the beginning of a conversation around two principles of CAS that have been lost in academia and mainstream animal rights (Nocella, George, Drew, Lupinacci, Ketenci, Purdy, & Leeson- Schatz, 2018; Socha & Blum, 2013). In simplest terms, to be radical is to start at the root of something, to see a problem and say, "Is it possible or desirable to throw out the worldview and conditions from which this problem arises? Do we rework what we've got, or do we start over?" In many ways, being radical is about finding ways to start over. This doesn't mean inventing something completely new. Beware of anyone who would claim to be able to accomplish such a feat. It is about exploring the tributaries of a river, rather than the main stream. We look forward to what we all will find converging in the margins.

References

Amster, R., DeLeon, A., Fernandez, L., Nocella, A. J., II, & Shannon, D. (2009). *Contemporary anarchist studies: An introductory anthology to anarchy in the academy.* New York, NY: Routledge.

Best, S., & Nocella, A. J., II (2004). *Terrorists or freedom fighters? Reflections on the liberation of animals.* New York, NY: Lantern Books.

Best, S., & Nocella, A. J., II (2006). *Igniting a revolution: Voices in defense of the Earth.* Oakland, CA: AK Press.

Best, S., Nocella, A. J., II, Kahn, R., Gigliotti, C., & Kemmerer, L. (2007). Introducing critical animal studies. *Journal of Critical Animal Studies, 5*(1), 4–5.

DeMello, M. (2013). *Animals and society: An introduction to human-animal studies.* New York, NY: Columbia University Press.

Freire, P. (1997). Pedagogy of the oppressed. New York, NY: Continuum Publishing Company.

Gandio, J., & Nocella, A. J., II (2014). *The terrorization of dissent: Corporate repression, legal corruption, and the Animal Enterprise Terrorism Act.* New York, NY: Lantern Books.

Nocella, A. J., II, Sorenson, J., Socha, K., & Matsuoka, A. (2013). *Defining critical animal studies: An intersectional social justice approach for liberation.* New York, NY: Peter Lang.

Nocella, A. J., II, White, R., & Cudworth, E. (2015). *Anarchism and animal liberation: Essays on complementary elements of total liberation.* Jefferson, NC: McFarland.

Nocella, A. J., II, George, A. E., Drew, C., Lupinacci, J., Ketenci, S., Purdy, I., & Leeson-Schatz, J. (2018). *Education for total liberation: Critical animal pedagogy and teaching against speciesism.* New York, NY: Peter Lang Publishing.

Nocella, A. J., II, & George, A. E. (2019). *Intersectionality of critical animal studies: A historical collection.* New York, NY: Peter Lang Books.

Nocella, A. J. II, Parson, S., George, A. E., & Eccles, S. (2019). *Historical scholarly collection of writings on the Earth Liberation Front.* New York, NY: Peter Lang Publishing.

Socha, K., & Blum, S. (2013). *Confronting animal exploitation: Grassroots essays on liberation and veganism.* Jefferson, NC: McFarland.

Waldau, P. (2013). *Animal studies: An introduction.* Oxford, UK: Oxford University Press.

1. Make-Believe Revolutions Make Make-Believe Revolutionaries

Kim Socha

I'm re-writing this chapter months after I first "finished" it. Back then it was called "My Year as a Radical Animal: Tales of Lies & Caution." However, after careful self-reflection, I decided to rewrite it for whatever audience is out there for anything I have to say about anything. I was honest about the facts in my previous iteration, but I wasn't honest about how I feel about those facts, not even to myself.

I was also trying to pose my chapter within a detached intellectual framework that made me sound more aloof than I am. Thus, instead of tales of a radical animal whose courage had no equal, I offer a semi-organized discourse by a sensitive, anxious, bourgie, failed revolutionary with my excuse for said failure being that there was no revolution to begin with, and I'm not sure I would have been brave enough to join if there had been.

In 2013, I co-edited an anthology called *Confronting Animal Exploitation* with my friend Sarahjane, an activist with a long history in the animal rights movement. At that time, I didn't have a long history, but I thought I knew it all with five years of veganism under my belt. Her chapter title in that book is "Some Things Get Better, Some Get Worse: On Being Scared, Being Around, and Trying to Be Kind." At the time, I found the title cumbersome, and I was wondering where she was going with it. Flash forward eight years, and I wish I could steal it as my own for this chapter. It pinpoints exactly how I feel. Leave it to Sarahjane.

A few years ago, I read an article about the closing of a vegan café that had introduced an 18% man tax one week per month in which men paid more than women to acknowledge the gender pay gap. The café also gave women priority seating. I liked this cheeky approach to feminism, and I appreciate that proceeds from "Man Tax Day" went to Aboriginal women. In the article, a social media poster is cited supporting the failed promise of the Handsome Her Café, stating, "As a vegan activist who went blindly and it turns out very naively into that role having no idea how much I would offend people by simply trying to make the world a better place I feel your frustration, your determination, and your resilience" (as cited in Smith, 2019, para. 19). That quote, much like Sarahjane's chapter title, pinpoints how I feel about my go as an animal rights activist.

I'm no longer surprised by just how much some people abhor those who pursue liberatory causes, especially animal liberation. Like the woman cited above, I have dealt with a fair amount of negative fallout because of my activism (more on that to come). I really was just trying to make the world a better place – *I swear*. The angry naysayers aren't the only ones to blame for what went wrong. My ego, and not the animals I advocated for, was driving some of my actions and rhetoric. I did and still do think I am right about how our fellow animal species should be treated, and I don't regret any of the actions I took to demonstrate that, except for those times when I *do* regret my actions. This ambivalence returns me to the promise of a revolution.

People in Black Smashing Things and Cuddling Animals Look Cool to Me

In books and lectures, I've oft told the story of how Shannon Keith's documentary *Behind the Mask: The Story of the People Who Risk Everything to Save Animals* (2006) made me go vegan. The undercover footage of animal abuse contained in that film, the kind I'd long avoided watching, horrified me. It led me to finally accept that all animals suffer when used as means to exploitative human ends, even the ones I liked to eat and wear. *Behind the Mask* was my bridge from vegetarianism to veganism to activism. My activism even included co-organizing a screening of Keith's other documentary *Skin Trade: Fur, Fashion, and Truth* (2010). I got the opportunity to tell her that her earlier film had made me go vegan. She was pretty nice.

Unintentionally, when talking about *Behind the Mask*, I almost always skipped mention of the true topic of the documentary – humans in balaclavas smashing things as they embark on missions to save animals from places of imprisonment and torture. I was 35 years old when I watched *Behind the Mask* in 2009, but I reacted to it like an impressionable youth watching badass video game characters doing rebellious things. ALF direct action takers laid the foundation of what I thought a real animal activist looked like. The sexiness of those classic ALF images isn't lost on modern culture creators

either, as proven by *Liberator*, a comic book series clearly inspired by stimu-
lating images like the ones from Keith's documentary.

How could there *not* be a revolution with such radical but kindhearted
people at the helm? We'll get to look cool dressed in black and breaking bad
people's things, but also kind as we cuddle those we've rescued from certain
death. I was hooked. And then I met some of the most famous ALF direct
action takers. Like Keith, some are nice, others are just there, and still others
are unrepentant predators who will not take accountability for their use of
violence and abuse against other humans. With heroes like this, I should have
seen cracks in the revolutionary veneer much sooner than I did. My bad for
seeking heroes.

I have never engaged in undercover action for animals, not really. I did
wear a lot of black and got a bunch of tattoos, though. That I can handle. For
a number of years, I muddled on with being an activist with images of the
ALF dancing in my mind, along with anarchic ideas from history's great philosophers and rebels that I'd read as part of my Ph.D. program. I was primed
to be a scholarly soldier in a revolution. But there was no revolution in the
way I imagined, and I was no well-trained soldier, and no one had prepared
me for what would become my own personal minefields: 1) my ego, 2) the
Internet, 3) liars, and 4) liars on the Internet.

"The Internet Ruins Everything"

Sarahjane and I toyed with the idea of writing another book in and around
2014/2015. Her part was going to be called "The Internet Ruins Everything."
As with her chapter from *Confronting Animal Exploitation*, I was perplexed.
The Internet, especially social media, was great! My only problem with it
was its potential to keep people from taking to the streets (*take that, key-
board warriors*). Otherwise, it was a forum to advocate for a world free from
violence to nonhuman animals. At the same time, I could use Facebook to
promote my various books (*take that, professor who scoffed that I took a job at
a community college and would never write again*) and other progressive projects (*take that, everyone who didn't think I was cool enough to be a revolutionary*). But then I made a teeny tiny name for myself in a microscopic nook of
the Internet, and I found out that the Internet does, indeed, ruin everything.
Sarahjane was right again.

I should have realized the Web's ruinous potential in the autumn of 2014
when a very short excerpt from my book *Animal Liberation and Atheism*
was published on the Friendly Atheist's *Patheos* page. The backlash in the
comments section was swift and not so friendly, with statements arising that

attacked me as a person ("crazy bitch" was one thoughtful gem) from those who could not have possibly read my book yet. Of course, there were positive commentators too, but then those supporting me or my book's premise were attacked as well. Despite this incident, I remained naïve about the Internet's destructiveness. I still believed in its awesome potential, so I continued on fairly uninhibitedly.

I like the British actor and free-thought advocate Stephen Fry. He's a great performer, thoughtful philosopher, and brilliant writer. So, rather than use my own words to explain how my views on the internet – or more specifically, social media – have changed since 2014, I liberally borrow from his explanation of why he left Twitter in 2016 (he's back now – another flawed hero):

> Oh goodness, what fun twitter was in the early days, a secret bathing-pool in a magical glade in an enchanted forest. It was glorious "to turn as swimmers into cleanness leaping." We frolicked and water-bombed and sometimes, in the moonlight, skinny-dipped. We chattered and laughed and put the world to rights and shared thoughts sacred, silly and profane. But now the pool is stagnant. It is frothy with scum, clogged with weeds and littered with broken glass, sharp rocks and slimy rubbish. If you don't watch yourself, with every move you'll end up being gashed, broken, bruised or contused. Even if you negotiate the sharp rocks you'll soon feel that too many people have peed in the pool for you to want to swim there anymore. The fun is over. (Fry, 2016, para. 2)

This paragraph eloquently summarizes how I now feel about the Internet, and even about activism, but only when activism encounters the Internet, as it inevitably does, because the "Internet ruins everything" and the "fun is over" now.

Along with thinking the Internet and social media were awesome, I thought the playing field was even. For this, I'm a hypocrite. Part of my fight for a better world has involved contesting injustice, especially the racial kind that poisons the United States. I took to the streets for Trayvon Martin, Michael Brown, and other Black Americans whose tragic murders highlighted just now much still needs to be done to confront racism. Back then, I would intellectualize on how "The System," "The State" does not operate fairly, but I didn't feel it in my gut because, as an educated, middle class, white woman, the world I navigate is generally kinder to me than it is to Black and Brown people. This is as true online as it is in real life, especially when gender is factored in. Amnesty International (2018) reports that "[w]omen of color . . . [are] 34% more likely to be mentioned in abusive or problematic tweets than white women" and "Black women were disproportionately targeted, being 84% more likely than white women to be mentioned in abusive or problematic tweets" (para. 6 & 7).

For this sad reality, I feel some gratitude for the injustices I experienced during my would-be revolutionary days. These were fleeting injustices that do not compare to racial inequities, but they helped me experience, rather than just know, that the world is unfair, people lie without compunction, and the justice system isn't a finely honed, fixed machine, but a Rube Goldberg gadget with moving, immovable, and removable parts.

I also had a hand, *and a heavy one at that*, in creating the imbroglios that I found myself in because I was kind of a troll before I even knew what that word meant, not a full-fledged troll, but troll-adjacent. I don't think I was a full-fledged troll because I didn't hide my identity or threaten people, mainly because I was so sure that my ethical stance absolved me from critique or counterattack. When I organized and participated in email and phone blockades, I identified who I was to the target(s) of the event, even leaving my phone number for people to call me back – they never did. There were two times when I used a non-identifiable email address, but not to threaten anyone, just to make the person or organization on the receiving end feel like more people were participating in the virtual blockade than actually were. That's not clever activism; it's just sad.

In my previous version of this chapter, I detailed three incidents from my "revolution" that turned me off to the Internet, especially social media, and to activism as a whole. In rereading that piece, I felt like I was putting myself in the role of victim in an ersatz way, like I was a badass warrior for animals, and everyone else just a punk. To be clear, I was on the receiving end of bad behavior, but I also don't like the way I behaved in these cases, even as I maintain, to this day, that I held the ethical upper hand from a theoretical perspective. Rather than rehash all the details, I have divided each incident into sections: Crime, Attempted Punishment, Actual Punishment, and Current Thoughts. I do this for myself more so than for the reader, but I'd be happy if someone gleans a lesson from my failed revolution.

Case 1 – Canceling a Cannibal?

- *Crime*: In 2015, I put a false review on Facebook of a restaurant in California that had started selling foie gras. In response, a chef who did not work at that restaurant went on an obscene Facebook tirade that attacked my age, appearance, and reproductive choices, along with threats to cook and eat me. Next, unbidden and unknown by me, fellow activists campaigned to get him fired, which he was in less than 24 hours.

- *Attempted Punishment:* The chef held me directly responsible for this outcome and sought to destroy my reputation, including a false assertion that I had posted a Facebook comment threatening his child – a comment I knew nothing about and would never have contemplated. To this day, I'm not sure if he made it up completely or was reacting to someone else.
- *Actual Punishment:* Barren of proof that I had threatened anyone, there was no punishment.
- *Current Thoughts*: I wish I hadn't posted a false review, not because of the ensuing attack, but because I have the ethical upper hand in any discussion of foie gras, so lies aren't necessary, and Facebook arguments are futile. I'm resentful of the activists who went after the chef without considering that I would be his target when the firing occurred. As to the chef, he said hurtful things, but I wasn't ever physically afraid of him. *No*, I didn't really think he was going to cook and eat me. I initially even felt bad that he was fired, but that was only until he accused me of threatening his daughter. I figured he's probably not a very good person if he would use his child as a "get-out-of-being-a-jerk-free" card. Or maybe he was just that scared and desperate to salvage his career. I'm more annoyed that people would believe something without a single shred of evidence – enter the Internet – except the words of a man who swore revenge on me on social media. A few people harassed me on Facebook for a while after this debacle. I assumed they were his friends, but if they weren't, it did bother me that someone thought I threatened a child. During the one time I tried to defend myself against the slander, I resorted to bringing up my volunteer work with youth. Like the chef, I used kids as the basis of my own "get-out-of-being-a-jerk-free" card, which is kind of funny, as is the idea of defending my character to strangers who had no interest in the truth. If they did, I wouldn't be defending myself to begin with. But people are starving to be outraged. Social media in a nutshell.

Case 2 – Book Breading

Part I

- *Crime*: At a morning protest in 2015, in front of witnesses and a police camera, I spray painted "scum" and "perv" on the sign of a dentist's office. "Scum" was in reference to his torturous killing of a supposedly protected lion in Zimbabwe; "perv" referred to the legally documented accusation that he sexually violated a woman when she was his patient and employee.

- *Attempted Punishment*: Felony, 10 years in prison! In truth, that punishment was never an option; rather, damage to property that costs over $1000 can theoretically result in such a sentence. But for a few people who anonymously emailed me, even that wouldn't have been enough. I really think they wanted me dead. Tortured, then dead.
- *Actual Punishment*: Gross misdemeanor, fine, 64 hours of community service, restitution, and two years of probation.
- *Current Thoughts*: There's a scene from *The Simpsons* where Bart is at a literary event and comes across a sign that says, "Book Reading." He takes out a can of spray paint and puts a "B" in front of the "R," making it state, "Book Breading." He starts to laugh mischievously but then the reality of how unimpressive his prank was sets in, so he shrugs, says "meh," and walks away. That's close to how I feel about my incursion into civil disobedience.

Part II

- *Crime*: I haven't a clue what my sin was here, but two of the women who took part in the spray paint incident were sisters from another state – and one of them had it in for me. I don't know why, as they had walked away without charges, putting all the blame on me, and I had taken full responsibility, never implicating them.
- *Attempted Punishment*: Destroy my reputation. *Here we go again!* As I sat in a jail cell, one of the released sisters began defaming me in a Facebook group. She said that she and/or her sister had been beat up while in the jail, and that I made it happen – not that I did it but that I must be responsible for one or both of them getting knocked around by someone they met while incarcerated. Upon my release, this same woman was in contact with the County Prosecutor saying I was defaming her on Facebook. I wasn't, and there was no evidence I was. Simultaneously, *she* was sending *me* threatening texts. When I pointed out that her texts prove she's the one making threats, she stopped. I never heard from her again.
- *Actual Punishment*: Nothing. This woman was so obviously unhinged that no one gave anything she said any credence, not the Prosecutor, not even the people in the Facebook group who live for that sort of drama.

- *Current Thoughts*: It would be easy for me to pontificate on how awful and silly that woman was, but I'd rather focus on my own awful silliness. I engaged in an unlawful act with two women I'd literally just met. I took part in a willful act of property destruction with no strategy or plan for follow through. I was so foolish that I almost deserved to have yet another person I didn't know try to ruin my life to save their own ass. Almost, but I don't think anyone deserves that. If you can be taken down because of the truth, so be it (though I hope there's always space for redemption). But to be taken down based on lies is intolerable to me.

This brings me to the situation that acted as the final nail in the coffin on which the tombstone reads: Kim's Animal Rights Revolution: R.I.P.

Case 3 – The Final Nail

- *Crime*: In 2015, as part of a wider campaign, I co-organized two-and-a-half demonstrations in the neighborhood of a university professor who engages in animal drug addiction experimentation; her husband is also a professor who uses animals in experiments.
- *Attempted Punishment*: An indefinite Restraining Order and 30 years in prison on terrorism charges for me and my six fellow activists! Okay, so I'm *really* exaggerating here, although the husband/professor did tell my co-organizer that he wanted her charged as a terrorist. In reality, we were charged with breaking an ordinance against residential picketing, which I think is a petty misdemeanor.
- *Actual Punishment*: The Restraining Order was dropped for all except me and my co-organizer. It remained in effect for two years. The prosecutor did not pursue the charge of breaking the ordinance, as I later explain.
- *Current Thoughts*: This could take a while . . .

I currently work in the field of violence prevention within families and between intimate partners. On a near daily basis, I listen to stories of how people abuse each other, and I offer them strategies for moving forward. My clients are from every gender and age group, from children to a woman who left her husband after a half century of physical abuse. The types of abuse I hear about are sadly familiar: physical, psychological, financial. More often, however, I'm hearing stories of legal abuse, a form of coercive control explained in an *Atlantic* article: "Many abusers misuse the court system to maintain power and control over their former or current part-ners, a method sometimes called 'vexatious' or 'abusive' litigation" (2019, Klein, para. 4). Klein goes on to explain that the "process [of responding to court documents] costs money and time, and can further traumatize victims" (para. 4.). I saw one client crushed by reading affidavits filled with lies meant to cast her as an unfit mother. Anyone can say anything in an affidavit, and it is taken as evidence. I believe it is psychologically abusive to lie about someone in a public forum, be it in a court document or on a social media platform, and people who want to hurt others know how effective this type of abuse is. I've learned this firsthand, as detailed above and now below.

It feels gross to be on the receiving end of a Restraining Order, and even grosser when you see lies about yourself therein. If I was given a Restraining Order based on what I really did, I would take it on the chin, as I did with my gross misdemeanor conviction, which impacted my life far greater than the Order.

At over $300 a head, my fellow activists and I bought the right to defend ourselves in civil court. (Actually, it was others in our community who con-tributed to our legal fund who allowed us this right, so much thanks to them.) It was worth it. First, five activists had their Orders dropped because they'd only attended one demonstration. Second, there is a legal record out there, via a court audio recording, confirming that that there is *no evidence* of the misdeeds my fellow activists and I were accused of. Rather, the judge's reason for the Order restraining me and the other organizer was that we had invaded the animal experimenters' privacy by revealing what they do for a living – even though everything they do is public record and, indeed, proudly touted on their university's Web site.

The judge, who I assume intended to keep the Order in place before our hearing even started, conceded that we never blocked the pair from leav-ing their home, we never published their home address, we didn't case their house, we didn't go to their front door pretending to be window salespeo-ple, we didn't scare neighborhood children, we didn't assault them, and we didn't damage their property. They accused us of things for which criminal charges could easily have been brought if there was a shred of truth to any of it. To this day, I'm stunned by the extent to which they were willing to lie, to paint us as criminal masterminds who can engage in nefarious deeds without leaving a trace of evidence behind (kind of like the chef did . . . and the out-of-state woman. Pattern!). As they depicted us, we were preternatural in our ability to threaten and terrify people with words and images that mag-ically disappear once uttered and shared. If we really were magical beings, we would have used our powers to save even one animal from being tortured in their labs. *Trust me.*

In reality, we were a group of activists ranging in age from 21 to 61 who showed up with banners depicting puppies, mice, and monkeys, and we chanted things like, "1, 2, 3, 4 . . . Open up the cage door! 5, 6, 7, 8 . . . Free the animals, liberate!" as we roamed about the tony neighborhood of two university professors. We didn't hide our names, faces, or the intentions of the event. We weren't sexy ALFers; we were cold Midwesterners.

And we were law-abiding citizens, as the police had sanctioned our first demonstration. They told us that as long as we didn't trespass on anyone's property, we were allowed to hold the event because the ordinance against picketing was "unconstitutional" – their word. I previously noted taking part in 2-and-a-*half* demonstrations in this neighborhood. The third and last one was cut short because the police changed their minds and said we'd be arrested if we didn't leave, so we left. Indeed, if they hadn't given us the green light the first time out, we likely would not have held the initial demo to begin with, and none of this would have happened. At the Restraining Order hearing, one of the police officers even begrudgingly acknowledged that he might have told us we could hold the initial protest.

To be clear, I don't think this was a complete set up, just a partial one. I think the cops thought we had a legal right to protest but then got in trouble for saying so. Before that third and final protest, they didn't meet us beforehand as they had previously because they wanted us to go back into the neighborhood and possibly be arrested. In fact, the animal experimenters demanded we be arrested, but the cops gave us a chance to leave first, which we did. (Hard not to wonder if this outcome would have been different if race had been a factor, especially in the state of Minnesota.)

My co-organizer and I were never tried for breaking the ordinance. Initially, the prosecutor offered us a favorable deal, the details of which I can't recall. What I do recall is that the offer was rescinded before we could accept because the animal experimenters felt we were being let off too easily. The new offer amounted to coercion. Tacked onto the deal was a clause that we agree to not oppose a continuation of the Restraining Order should they apply for a new one within the next five years. If we did not accept, two more charges would be added – one count of misdemeanor disorderly conduct and one of gross misdemeanor stalking. There are no honest or logical definitions of the words "disorderly conduct" or "stalking" that describe the actions we took during this campaign.

This is an important lesson for any would-be revolutionaries: With the stroke of a prosecutor's pen, a protestor against cruelty to animals can become a stalker and/or rioter . . . for a protest that the police said could be held. We'd even brought our own legal observer to the first event because we wanted to do everything by the book. Again, please hear this: *There is no book*. With this reality laid bare, my co-defendant and I accepted a continuance for dismissal, meaning we didn't have to make a plea of guilt or non-guilt only to the initial charge of breaking the ordinance, a charge which eventually disappears from the official record. In terms of legal outcomes, it is a good resolution second only to having charges dropped immediately. If we hadn't had a radical lawyer willing to take on all of our cases free-of-charge, all seven of us would have had no chance of pursing justice.

I'm still irritated about what happened. I'm mad at the expected targets but also at myself, maybe more so at myself. I should have known that the police aren't inherently trustworthy and that the justice system is not about truth but about the ability to sell a narrative of the truth. But on some level, I felt those rules didn't apply to me. Is that privileged thinking? Sure. Is that an ego run amok? Likely. And truth be told, I wasn't all innocence and sweetness during my revolution. I was petty. I was puerile. I posted goofy videos and pictures on social media trying to look like the rad activist while mocking others. It became more about me than the animals in those cases. I am disappointed by some of my behaviors during that time.

These days, I'm ambivalent about home/neighborhood demonstrations. It seems like the ultimate form of trolling. Even though I had a message of compassion, there is an intrinsic hostility to entering someone's neighborhood to protest their behavior. I comfort myself with the awareness that I never threatened anyone, never hid my face or intentions, and that people who do bad things should at the very least be irritated from time to time.

But where does that end when the issue is not that most people are doing the wrong thing but that they are doing what they deem the right thing? Those who knowingly and enjoyably enact evil deeds are a small proportion of the population. Then there's the rest of us. Professor 1 engages in life-changing research to help ease the burden of millions of drug addicts. Professor 2 has dedicated her life to freeing primates from situations of abuse, pain, and isolation. Professor 1 tortures animals for a living on the tax-payer's dime. Professor 2 stalks other professors during her free time, terrorizing neighborhood children in the process.

Make no mistake, I'm not posing moral relativism here. I am against the use of animals in medical and scientific research, and, as a former cocaine addict, I'm especially appalled by animal addiction studies. My questions are not about what is ethically just but about what one effectively does to remedy injustice. They are questions about strategies, narratives, not morality and ethics. My "revolutionary" responses make me feel like I waded through a urine filled pool into which I too oft unloaded my own heavy bladder. Most importantly, I don't have tangible evidence that I have ever done anything to actually liberate an animal from a lab, as can those who count themselves as Animal Liberation Front participants. Perhaps if I could, my opinion of my revolution would be different.

Conclusion

This is a hard chapter to conclude because I'm not sure what lessons to pull from it. I don't want to dissuade anyone from taking unconventional action for animals, but I don't want to foster romantic falsehoods about it either. I want you to know what the ramifications might be if you color outside the lines. I want you to know how much power you have but that the people who hurt animals usually have more power than you, and if they take you to court, they have a good chance of winning. And when the revolution ends, you may have to bear the consequential burdens of a criminal record. I also want you to know how willing people are to lie baldly and boldly (and, at times, badly) if it means saving their proverbial bottoms.

I asked someone close to me to read this chapter. He liked it okay but was disappointed by the initial conclusion, noting that I sounded like a "jaded nihilist," while he had been looking for inspiration. He also reminded me of a talk I once gave telling animal activists not to surrender to the fear of repercussions because they (the animals) are more afraid than we are. *Yikes.* I had no comeback other than I don't want to lie about my experiences, so an honest account of my year as a "radical" seemed more meaningful than a contrived story of bravado. I am still in the animal rights and liberation movement, but quietly, almost invisibly, so. I still believe in everything I believed back when I was "raising hell," and I still support the ethos of the Animal Liberation Front, but I have become more thoughtful about concepts such as strategy, optics, collaboration, and how best to use anger and ego – those most powerful and amazing tools that we all carry with us to ours and others benefits and/or detriments. Perhaps that is the lesson then? Not whether to be active, but how to be so more strategically and perhaps more effectively.

I will end with that positive thought because I'm not a jaded nihilist but an optimistic one. This chapter has been a long gripe about how the "storming the Bastille style" revolution I had planned never came to fruition. But social change does not have a deadline, much less one imposed by my activist impatience. Change does happen though – all the time and all through time – and we all contribute to it, consciously and unconsciously, in small ways and big. This is a good thing because it means a revolution may still be on its way, and there is a lot we can get done during this time, what I like to see as the early days of a worldscape built upon conceptions of compassion, peace, and parity for all sentient beings, not just bipedal ones.

Doesn't get more optimistic than that.

References

Amnesty International (2018). Troll patrol findings. *Decoders.amnesty.org*. Retrieved from https://decoders.amnesty.org/projects/troll-patrol/findings

Fry, S. (2016, February 15). Too many people have peed in the pool. *StephenFry.com*. Retrieved from http://www.stephenfry.com/2016/02/peedinthepool/

Klein (2019, July 18). How domestic abusers weaponized the courts. *The Atlantic*. Retrieved from https://www.theatlantic.com/family/archive/2019/07/how-abusers-use-courts-against-their-victims/593086/

Smith, R. (2019, April 25). Melbourne cafe Handsome Her closing two years after introducing 'man tax.' *New Zealand Herald*. Retrieved from https://www.nzherald.co.nz/lifestyle/news/article.cfm?c_id=6&objectid=12225208

2. Listening to and Learning from Leftist Critiques of Animal Liberation

WILL BOISSEAU

> His theme is Exploitation: the rich Few
> Battening on labour of the Many. True—
> But look within his larder. Will he dine
> Himself on limbs of slaughtered sheep and kine?
> Are those poor sufferers not exploited too?
> Henry Salt, The Socialist Not a Vegetarian, 1928

This chapter considers the engagement of radical animal liberationists with wider socialist, leftist and trade union movements. The chapter takes its starting point by considering the activism and propaganda of Henry Salt, an anarchist-inspired socialist who developed a total liberation perspective during the work of the Humanitarian League, which formed in 1891 in England. As we see, Salt linked human and non-human animal exploitation and aimed to develop class analysis, which he developed from studying and translating Marx, to include other animals. It is interesting for leftist animal activists to notice that Salt faced many of the same arguments against his animal advocacy that are presented in current leftist critiques of veganism and animal liberation. The chapter therefore considers hostility towards activism for animals in the British socialist movement at the turn of the twentieth century and current leftist arguments against veganism and animal liberation. Considering these arguments helps leftist animal activists listen to and learn from our comrades as we attempt to build solidarity alliances which respect the intersecting struggles against human and animal oppression. The final section of the chapter considers current avenues for radical animal activists to show solidarity with other leftist movements whilst highlighting, as Salt did, the class politics of animal oppression. One caveat is that although we can learn from our movement's history and the struggles that leftist animal advocates have fought in the past, the real work of movement building comes from engaging with those in struggle against different forms of racial, gender and class oppression today. As Angela Davis (2017) explains, forward looking social justice movements should

> recognize that universal freedom is an ideal best represented not by those who are already at the pinnacle of racial, gender and class hierarchies but rather by those whose lives are most defined by conditions of unfreedom and by ongoing struggles to extricate themselves from those conditions (p. xiv).

I do not claim that Salt lays down a blue print that current animal liberationists should follow. As a straight, white, middle class (Eton educated) male, Salt's perspective was limited by the class, race and gender conditioning of his time. Clearly, theory and activism by those at the forefront of gender, racial and class oppression have been at the vanguard of grounding animal liberation as radical non-hierarchical praxis that has made animal liberation a radical social movement, in particular ecofeminists and black feminists who developed intersectional theory.

I believe that it is particularly important to consider the leftist critiques presented in this chapter because movements grow from being self-critical, assessing our successes and learning from our failures. The chapter draws from a range of primary material, and the inspiration for considering this topic stems from interviews I have conducted with over fifty animal activists about their theory and tactics.

Henry Salt and Socialist Animal Advocacy

Keith Tester's (1991) claim that Henry Salt, who founded the Humanitarian League in 1891, 'more or less invented animal rights' is aimed at dismissing the animal rights movement, rather than praising Salt (p. 194). The animal rights movement has a lineage dating to philosophers such as Pythagoras or the growth of Jainism, Buddhism and Hinduism (Kemmerer & Nocella, 2011). However, the ideas that have shaped the current radical animal liberation movement and were developed by Critical Animal Studies scholar-activists, including total liberation politics, do have a concrete foundation in the British socialist movement and in particular in the work of Salt and the Humanitarian League. Indeed, when Peter Singer (originally published 1975; 2005) wrote *Animal Liberation*, he was able to explain that his ideas 'had all been said before' by Salt (p. xvi). It was due to the leftist influence of Salt that Singer described the animal rights movement as a 'liberation movement [that] is a demand for an end to prejudice and discrimination based on an arbitrary characterisation' (xii). Although Singer's utilitarian welfarist position has been criticised and updated by more recent scholars who want to see abolitionist outcomes, Singer's comments show that Salt was regarded by some as a key figure in the development of animal rights theory.

Salt himself was tireless in propagating the socialist and vegetarian message (the word 'vegan' was not coined until 1944); however, despite the accolades from Singer and Tester, Salt and the Humanitarian League were largely ridiculed by leftists in Britain and later forgotten. As the twentieth century progressed, a movement 'devoted to the art of being kind' seemed somewhat out of place within the industrial and political labour movement that focused on class politics and industrial action. One British trade union representing workers in the meat industry argued in 1923 that 'the advocates of the humane-killer have captured the sentimentalists in our movement, but the Trade Unions are not sentimental bodies' (Trade Union Congress, 1923, p. 394). The Humanitarian League were accused of being 'sentimental' because alongside animal rights and anti-vivisection, they campaigned against capital punishment, the arms trade, and for colonial freedom. Sentimentalism can be seen as connected to total liberation because it relies on an ethic of caring and this ethic of care is expanded to all humans, animals and the Earth.

In Salt's life and work, we can see the development of the anarchist concept of total liberation. Salt (1921) believed that

> the emancipation of [humanity] from cruelty and injustice will bring with it in due course the emancipation of animals also ... [T]he two reforms are inseparably connected, and neither can be fully realized alone (p. 122).

Salt (1921) developed a concept of 'intermingled injustices' in which he argued that

> all great issues of justice or injustice are crossed and intermingled, so that no one cruelty can be singled out as the source of all other cruelties, nor can any one reform be fully realized apart from the rest (p. 132).

He directly linked the treatment and exploitation of non-human animals in the meat industry to the lives of the working class exploited by capitalism. Salt (1889) argued that the masses lived lives of 'unremitting toil' in 'much the same' way as 'countless numbers of harmless animals' were 'condemned to torture and death' (para. 3). To Salt, 'humanity ... must apply, not to mankind alone, but to all sentient life' (para. 4). Indeed, for Salt, 'A Vegetarian ... cannot consistently be an opponent of a system which holds out a prospect of relief to the victims of the sweater's den', meaning sweatshop factory workers, and 'a Socialist . . . ought not to be able to regard with complacency the horrible traffic in flesh' (ibid).

Salt (1908) went further than insisting that the working class should show compassion for animals. Instead he argued that as 'the labour of animals has been interwoven with the labour of man [sic] in the fabric of human society, it seems wiser to claim for animals their due rights, as a part of that organisation': members of the working class (para. 25). To Salt (1921), animals were members of an exploited and oppressed class just like the workers; similarly the bourgeoisie were 'almost literally cannibals, as devouring the flesh and blood of the higher non-human animals . . . and indirectly cannibals, as living by the sweat and toil of the classes who do the hard work of the world' (p. 64).

Salt did not simply aim to protect the oppressed, but to create a beautiful society where compassion and social justice could flourish. There was simply no room in a 'community possessed of true refinement' for the 'degrading and disgusting institutions as the slaughter-house and the butcher's shop' (Salt, 1896, para. 3). Salt's concept of animal rights fits the current approach of the radical animal liberation movement. In nineteenth century Britain, Salt developed the concepts of total liberation and intermingled injustices (though they certainly had already materialised in other cultures). Salt linked his animal advocacy to a rejection of all social hierarchies, which he saw as interconnected. Despite the theoretical work linking animal abuse to human exploitation under capitalism and in class society, Salt was unable to convince socialists of his day to join the cause. In kind, the next section looks at arguments against animal advocacy from British socialists who disagreed with Salt's philosophy.

Socialist Arguments Against Animal Liberation

When Salt and his comrades in the Humanitarian League presented their ideas that human and animal oppressions were fundamentally linked and must be tackled simultaneously, they were met with laughter and derision amongst many of the British left. This is interesting for our current movement because we can see in this historical instance the kinds of arguments that have traditionally been stacked against us, and how we can build solidarity with leftist movements today.

Salt's animal advocacy message was attacked by many socialists, including Henry Hyndman, an authoritarian Marxist who founded the Social Democratic Federation in 1881, which was the first socialist party in Britain. Hyndman, who claimed to be a 'scientific socialist', calculated that the intervention in the socialist movement by vegetarians like Henry Salt, George Bernard Shaw and Edward Carpenter had 'put us back twenty years at least' (as cited in Winsten, 1951, p. 64). Hyndman's antipathy to socialist animal advocates was not on moral grounds, but was because such concerns would make socialists appear out of touch, and thus unable to influence the working class. Hyndman wrote that: 'I do not want the movement to be a depository of odd cranks: humanitarians, vegetarians, anti-vivisectionists and anti-vaccinationists, arty-crafties and all the rest of them. We are scientific socialists and have no room for sentimentalities' (ibid). It should be noted here that Hyndman refused to engage animal advocates on moral grounds, and instead attempted to distract attention from the issue by arguing that it would not be popular amongst the British working class. It is also troubling that Hyndman linked animal advocacy with '*all the rest of them*' which could be a bigoted attack on the gay liberation movement and the free love practiced by Edward Carpenter and others (Rowbotham, 2008).

It is also possible that Hyndman's hostility stemmed from the antagonistic attitude of the first animal welfare societies towards the working class; for instance, the Royal Society for the Protection of Cruelty to Animals was seen as 'a middle-class body defining itself against the lowest classes who tortured animals for sport' (Kean, 1998, p. 36). Early animal welfare groups aimed to 'civilize' the working class by opposing bull-baiting and cock-fighting alongside an opposition to drinking and gambling. Hyndman believed that the 'older humanitarians' had a patronizing attitude because they 'regarded the object of its compassion whether the "lower orders" or the "lower animals" with a charitable eye' (cited in Winsten, 1951, p. 65). Unlike current radical animal activists who embrace the concept of total liberation and believe that all forms of oppression are interconnected and must be simultaneously opposed, Hyndman believed that focusing on animal issues would detract time and energy which could be dedicated to the class struggle.

Whilst one might presume that authoritarian Marxists would reject animal advocacy (because this is still the case today), it is disappointing to learn that Salt also faced hostility from anarchistic libertarian socialists surrounding the Socialist League and *Commonweal*: the League's paper declared that 'vegetarianism was an employers' plot to force workers to accept a lower standard of living' (Rowbotham, p. 97). William Morris (cited in Salmon, 1996) wrote that vegetarian-socialists 'make themselves liable to the sneer of an anti-socialist acquaintance of mine, who said to me one day, "All you Socialists have each of you another fad besides Socialism"' (p. 140). Morris believed that there was something suspiciously authoritarian in trying to dictate other people's eating habits; he wrote that vegetarians 'would be as tyrannical as other ascetics if they had the chance' (ibid). Morris seemed unaware of the possible health and economic benefits of a vegan diet when he wrote: 'a man can hardly be a sound socialist who puts forward vegetarianism as a solution of the difficulties between labour and capital ... as one may think very severe capitalists may like to do, if the regime was not applied to themselves' (ibid).

Morris was not entirely dismissive of vegetarianism; however, he prioritized improving the current conditions of the working class. As Colin Spencer (2000) notes, ideologically motivated veganism or vegetarianism can only flourish when people have 'enough income to afford an abundance of food, so that some foods might be sacrificed' (p. 276). Similarly, in 1888, Morris wrote that he could accept simplicity of life, including vegetarianism, 'so long as it is voluntary; but surely there is enough involuntary simplicity of life' (pp. 467–468). Morris argued that a nation-wide dietary change would not benefit the working class, who would still receive insufficient nourishment:

> If our whole capitalistic society were to become vegetarian together the "poor", i.e, the producers, would be forced to live upon vegetarian cag-mag, while the rich, i.e, the proprietary class, live upon vegetarian dainties (ibid).

This argument left scope for a future vegetarian regime, as a 'society of equals', which Morris believed would one day come to fruition and would be better placed to make informed dietary choices. Until then, Morris would continue to demand 'roast meat' rather than 'skilly without the cheese' for the workers (ibid, p. 267). Whilst workers lived poorly by necessity, Morris asked vegetarian reformists not to '*evade* the real question: Why are we not a society of equals?' (ibid, p. 468).

Responding to criticism made in the Socialist League publication *Commonweal* in 1896, Salt seemed genuinely pained that certain socialists would 'devote their superfluous energies' to an attack on animal rights (para. 1). Rather than responding to the attack in kind, Salt maintained that animal advocacy could be thought of merely as an 'important accessory consideration' to the fundamental economic and political changes that would be brought about through a social revolution (para. 2). Salt felt that socialists should not ignore an argument built upon a consideration of justice and humanity, for those are the very principles which he believed socialists and animal activists should share.

The modern radical animal liberation movement can learn a lot from Salt and the Humanitarian League. For instance, like Salt, animal activists should root their animal activism in class politics and the interconnected systems of oppression. Animal activists today might highlight global food poverty and the effects of the meat and dairy industry on climate catastrophe. Like Salt, animal activists should not be apologetic about their revolutionary agenda as we aim to create better societies where animals, humans and the planet can live with dignity. Salt found himself engaging in antagonistic arguments with people who had no real moral objection to animal rights, but found various excuses such as other issues (like the class struggle) being more significant. In this instance, Salt was prepared to build solidarity alliances by drawing on common goals with other socialists. Salt recognised that animal activism wasn't at the centre of all struggles, but built an invitational approach which offered solidarity without demands. The Humanitarian League supported social justice issues without the expectation that participants in those struggles would become vegans or support animal activism.

Current Leftist Critiques of Vegan Outreach

In this section, I briefly consider current leftist critiques of veganism and animal liberation. These critiques of veganism and animal activism are important because radical animal liberationists must listen to and learn from other leftists in order to help build a social movement for Earth, animal and human liberation. This section focuses on the vegan advocacy movement because it is here that the clearest and most relevant criticisms emerge, even from those within the radical animal liberation movement. For instance, Steven Best (2014) argues that vegan activists live

> in a deep state of denial and delusion about the urgency of ecological crisis and [are] dangerously naive in [their] faith in the singular efficacy of conjectural education and moral persuasion apart from direct action, mass confrontation, civil disobedience, alliance politics, and struggle for radical change (p. 45).

Further, Josée Johnston (2008) links the critique of veganism to a lack of class analysis within the animal liberation movement. Johnston writes that

> this particular framing of the citizen-consumer hybrid – as a chance to feel morally correct through shopping – creates a contradiction in terms of class politics. A close examination of the moral implications of the citizen-consumer hybrid reveals that it creates a hierarchy of moral stratification that maps onto class stratification, thereby lending more weight to consumerism versus citizenship (p 256).

These passages from Best and Johnston show that the contemporary vegan movement has often been insular and narrowly focused on increasing consumer choices for vegans. This is dangerous because the market for veganism has been in high priced products which creates a wealth barrier to the

supposedly ethical consumer choices. The lack of connection between veganism and other social justice issues has meant that currently mainstream
veganism is not helping to bring about a movement for total liberation.

The leftist critiques broadly encompass three areas: firstly, that veganism
does not provide a challenge to capitalism; secondly, that veganism stresses
social change through activist's involuntary role as consumers; finally, that
vegans are authoritarian or elitist in regarding veganism as a 'moral baseline'
that everyone should adopt.

No Challenge to Capitalism

The term 'leftist critique' is not intended to imply that these assessments
come from outside the animal liberation movement. Although some criticisms come from anarchists and socialists who are unsupportive of animal advocacy, animal activists are also aware of the challenges they face. In
particular, animal activists are aware that veganism does not automatically
present a challenge to capitalism. As lauren Ornelas, founder of the Food
Empowerment Project, argues, there is nothing inherently ethical about non-
animal products:

> From vegan chocolate coming from West Africa that is laden with slavery and
> the worst forms of child labor to the plight of farm workers in the fields who
> pick our produce, we all need to recognise the impact that our food choices have
> on others (as cited in Adams & Gruen, 2014, p. 33).

Vegan activists are aware of this dilemma; some activists try to balance the
changes they ultimately wish to see with their everyday existence, striving
to do the least harm and live with minimal cruelty whilst daring to dream
of the eradication of capitalism. Many activists believe that there is also a
danger that capitalism will create a niche market for vegan products which
allows activists to 'play in the corner' without effecting any fundamental
changes. Capitalism has the ability to absorb and remarket oppositional
ideas. This is the case with many elements of the environmental movement which use anarchist 'ideas as a critical touchstone and resource for
inspiration' but have accepted a 'green market economy' which 'entails the
rejection of ideas that are determined by the anarchist goal of complete
abolition of the state' (de Geus, 1996, pp. 205–206). Of course, there are
many people who follow a vegan diet, including those who adopt veganism for health reasons, who have no desire to challenge capitalism or seek
wider systemic changes. Radical animal liberationists must challenge this
by always putting an anti-capitalist agenda at the heart and centre of their
veganism.

Individual Role as Consumers

Some leftists dismiss veganism as a mere consumer activity (Gelderloos, 2011). David Nibert (2002, 2013) believes that promoting veganism as a solution to animal abuse undermines building a social movement for animal liberation because it focuses on the individual instead of the collective. Nibert believes that focusing on the structures of society, including an opposition to capitalism, should be at the center of the vegan project. For Nibert, vegan activists are wrong to focus exclusively on the notion of speciesism because it makes animal abuse appear to be an individual prejudice rather than a result of structural and economic forces. Animal activists have responded to the dismissal of veganism as an insignificant consumer choice by highlighting their opposition to capitalism, which is 'the totalitarianism of economics over life. All life becomes a commodity in this society' (*Arkangel*, No. 16, undated, p. 33). For these activists, veganism is an attempt to disrupt the commodity fetishism that turns other animals in to consumable products.

Radical animal activists recognise that simply becoming vegan will not bring an end to capitalism, because all food is currently produced within the capitalist system. Of course, activists do not limit their analysis to a critique of capitalism alone; many also consider 'the ways in which, for example, the intersection of colonialist and patriarchal relations is particularly marked in the farming of animals for food' (Cudworth, 2014, p. 30). Instead of dismissing all personal lifestyle changes as irrelevant, radical vegan activists seek to balance their own moral choices with efforts to bring about wider social change, for instance by participating in Food Not Bombs chapters that save vegan and vegetarian food from being discarded and distribute it to the public as a way of protesting against poverty and war.

Moral Baseline

The last criticism of veganism is that, in demanding that veganism act as a moral baseline, the use of the diet becomes elitist. This leads to a number of problems for animal activists, including a potentially self-congratulatory attitude, a dismissal of vegetarianism and a belief that animal liberation is the 'final frontier' of discrimination. This criticism ties in with the unfairly perpetuated idea that vegans 'see themselves as better than non-vegans, morally superior, preachy, and even annoying' (Gruen, p. 133). It seems clear from discussions in animal rights magazines such as *Arkangel* that *some* vegan activists believe that they hold the 'moral high ground' and that veganism is a superior lifestyle to meat eating. Peter Gelderloos (2005) argues that such a self-congratulatory attitude in a social movement is potentially damaging not only because 'occupying the moral high ground necessarily entails the creation of an inferior "other" to oppose' but also because the success of protest groups requires constant assessment and self-criticism, and such evaluation will be blocked if a movement is always determined to appear morally wholesome (p. 49, p. 61). One correspondent to the *S.A.R.P [Support Animal Rights' Prisoners] Newsletter* (1991) believed that 'if we are morally superior through our beliefs then any action carried out in the furtherance of those beliefs cannot be morally wrong' (p. 3).

The belief that veganism should be a moral baseline is also liable to divide the animal rights movement and prevent alliances with other social justice issues. Firstly, vegan activists can be inexplicably hostile to vegetarians whom they perceive as hypocritical or ignorant. For instance, Kevin Watkinson and Donald O'Driscoll (2014) argue that

> [v]egetarianism doesn't challenge the paradigm of exploitation. Some people transition to veganism through vegetarianism, whilst others believe they are doing something useful to help animals, but instead merely enforce the property status of animals.

Some vegan activists have claimed that animal liberation must be seen as the moral imperative of our time, and that because animal liberation 'covers *all* abuse and exploitation. It is the *ultimate* freedom movement, the "final frontier"' (Webb, 2004). Such claims are clearly liable to alienate other social justice campaigners who would see no reason why other causes should be subsumed by animal liberation because it 'covers *all* abuse', and will be hostile to the suggestion that animal rights is the 'final frontier' when other frontiers of discrimination affect the daily lives of millions of humans.

There are three ways that radical animal activists have addressed leftist critiques: firstly, activists have highlighted that 'it is not possible to be "pure" without collaborating with the current unjust system' and so such a baseline cannot exist (Watkinson, O'Driscoll, p. 17); secondly, vegan activists have focused on the oppression of human workers in food production, which means that 'seen through an intersectional lens, vegan choices can certainly still be bound up in various forms of exploitation' (Twine, 2014, pp. 192–193); finally, vegan activists have decided to 'forgo top-down universalizing judgements' and instead they promote an invitational approach of 'contextual moral veganism' that recognises 'contextual exigencies' that may affect one's dietary choices (Gruen, p. 130). It is also important to highlight that veganism is an intersectional theory and not simply a dietary choice because through intersectional theory animal activists can build a movement for total liberation which supports human, animal and Earth liberation.

Listening and Learning

It is vital that radical animal liberationists listen to and learn from leftist critiques of our movement, for in this way we can build solidarity alliances and strengthen our theory, tactics and direct actions. Learning from leftist critiques, both from the socialist movement in the early part of the twentieth century and today, it is important that radical animal activists do the following:

- *Highlight the intersections of systems of oppression.* This should be done by learning from those with lived experience at the interface of class, gender and race oppressions. Radical animal liberation activists can play a supportive role, when invited, in these movements. This can occur in supporting feminist initiatives that provide safe spaces for victims of domestic abuse and their companion animals. Radical animal liberationists might also highlight the interconnections between animal and Earth liberation by engaging in environmental direct action including transition networks and community gardening. Even within the animal liberation movement, activists should resist the prominence of white male figureheads and leaders and instead listen to and learn from activists within the movement who are engaged in daily struggles against other forms of oppression.
- *Emphasise class politics.* Animal activists must remember that there is no ethical consumerism within capitalism, and that the agency of humans and animals is greatly diminished under capitalism. As Henry Salt said, humans and other animals are exploited in much the same way under class society. Radical animal activists can highlight this connection by supporting workers who are exploited by the animal industrial complex. For instance, they can support restaurant, delivery and fast food workers demanding a living wage and collective bargaining rights. One example of such a campaign are the McLibel activists who highlighted the unethical targeting of children, exploitation of workers, animal cruelty, and damage to the environment carried out by McDonalds as well as focusing on the global domination of corporations. The activists were sued by the global fast food giant in 1990 and subsequent trial proceedings took 15 years.
- *Adopt an invitational approach.* One traditional criticism of animal liberation is that it is totalitarian in approach and elitist in practice. Animal liberationists can avoid this by engaging in invitational campaigns in their workplaces, communities and trade unions. These

campaigns can be spontaneous, fun and relate to other local issues. For instance, vegan trade unionists could highlight the issue of people working unpaid overtime without taking lunch breaks by providing regular vegan meals for co-workers.

- *Practice solidarity without demands.* Radical animal activists will try and be good allies with other social justice movements not as a way of promoting veganism but because they believe in the aims of these movements. On these occasions, animal liberationists will show solidarity without expecting members of other social movements to suddenly forego meat and dairy in return. This could include providing vegan meals at sights of anarchy in action such as picket lines or protest sites.
- *Be unapologetic and radical.* Animal liberationists want to completely transform society. We are anti-capitalist revolutionaries who want to live without hierarchy and oppression. When animal liberationists picture the world we want to live in, it is not a world where countless animals are killed in brutal and demeaning conditions. When engaging with other leftists, we should be unapologetic about our radical vision of a world without exploitation.
- *Remember that actions speak louder than words.* When forming solidarity alliances, actions always speak louder than words, *including the words in this chapter.*

The work of alliance building through listening, learning and engaging with comradely criticism is vital for radical animal liberationists because such solidarity work helps build progressive alliances and practically demonstrates total liberation politics. Animal activists who engage in leftist politics may remember David Pellow's (2014) assertion that

> social change is messy, and that notion should be both humbling and emboldening: there is a great deal of work to be done, so there must be many forms of activism and types of activist (p. 255)

A growing number of animal activists believe that it is vital to build alliances across social justice movements. To build these alliances, activists must 'understand that one will get into conflicts and learn about others' (Nocella, 2010, p. 182). These activists know that alliance politics come 'from a place of respect that carries out listening projects and healing and transformative activities' (ibid, p. 183). It is important to recognise that conflicts will emerge, both between social movements and within the animal advocacy movement, but that 'everyone need not agree and should not agree, lest society become an ideological cemetery' (Bookchin, 1999, p. 149). Through the messy work of listening to and learning from our comrades in other social justice movements, we can continue to fight for a world where all are free.

References

Adams, C. J., & Gruen, L. (Eds.). (2014). *Ecofeminism: Feminist intersections with other animals and the Earth.* London: Bloomsbury.

Arkangel, No. 16. Undated, p. 33

Best, S. (2014). *The politics of total liberation: Revolution for the 21st century.* Basingstoke: Palgrave Macmillan.

Bookchin, M. (1999). *Anarchism, Marxism, and the future of the left: Interviews and essays, 1993–1998.* Edinburgh: AK Press.

Cudworth, E. (2014). Beyond speciesism: Intersectionality, critical sociology and the human domination of other animals. In N. Taylor & R Twine (Eds.), *The rise of critical animal studies: From the margins to the centre.* London: Routledge.

Davis, A. (2017). Forward. In P. Khan-Cullors & A. Bandele (Eds.), *When they call you a terrorist: A black lives matter memoir.* Edinburgh, Cannongate.

de Geus, M. (1996). The ecological restructuring of the state. In B. Doherty & M. de Geus (Eds.), *Democracy and green political thought: Sustainability, rights and citizenship.* London: Routledge.

Gelderloos, P. (2005). *How nonviolence protects the state.* The Anarchist Library. Retrieved from http://theanarchistlibrary.org/library/peter-gelderloos-how-nonviolence-protects-the-state

Gelderloos, P. (2011). *Veganism: Why not: An anarchist perspective.* The Anarchist Library. Retrieved from https://theanarchistlibrary.org/library/peter-gelderloos-veganism-why-not

Gruen, L. (2014). Facing death and practicing grief. In C. J. Adams & L. Gruen (Eds.), *Ecofeminism: Feminist intersections with other animals and the earth.* London: Bloomsbury.

Johnston, J. (2008). The citizen-consumer hybrid: Ideological tensions and the case of whole foods market. *Theory and Society,* 37, 229–270.

Kean, H. (1998). *Animal rights: Political change in Britain since 1800.* London: Reakton Books.

Kemmerer, L., & Nocella, A. J., II (Eds.). (2011). *Call to compassion: Religious perspectives on animal advocacy.* New York: Lantern Books.

Morris, W., & Salmon, N. (Eds.). (1996). *Journalism, contributions to commonweal, 1885–1890.* Bristol: Thoemmes Press.

Nibert, D. (2002). *Animal rights/Human rights: Entanglements of oppression and liberation.* Plymouth: Rowman & Littlefield.

Nibert, D. (2013). *Animal oppression & human violence: Domesecration, capitalism and global conflict*. New York: Columbia University Press.

Nocella, A. J., II (2010). Abolition a multi-tactical movement strategy. *Journal for Critical Animal Studies, 8*(1–2), 176–183.

Pellow, D. N. (2014). *Total liberation: The power and promise of animal rights and the radical earth movement*. Minneapolis: University of Minnesota Press.

Rowbotham, S. (2008). *Edward Carpenter: A life of liberty and love*. London: Verso.

S.A.R.P Newsletter, No. 5. November 1991, p. 3.

Salt, H. S. (1889). Vegetarianism 'As she is spoke'. *The Vegetarian, 11*(27), July 6. Retrieved from https://www.henrysalt.co.uk/library/essay/vegetarianism-as-she-is-spoke/

Salt, H. S. (1896). Socialists and vegetarians. *To-Day*, November 1896. Retrieved from https://www.henrysalt.co.uk/library/essay/socialists-and-vegetarians/

Salt, H. S. (1908). Have animals rights? *Humane Review*, January 1908, Vol. 8. Retrieved from https://www.henrysalt.co.uk/library/essay/have-animals-rights/

Salt, H. S. (1921). *Seventy years among savages*. London: George Allen & Unwin.

Singer, S. (2005). *Animal liberation* (2nd ed.). London: Pimlico.

Spencer, C. (2000). *Vegetarianism: A history*. London: Grub Street.

Tester, K. (1991). *Animals and society: The humanity of animal rights*. London: Routledge.

Trade Union Congress, *Trade Union Congress Report*, (1923). London: TUC.

Twine, R. (2014). Ecofeminism and veganism: Revisiting the question of universalism. In C. J. Adams & L. Gruen (Eds.), *Ecofeminism: Feminist intersections with other animals and the earth*. London: Bloomsbury.

Watkinson, K., & O'Driscoll, D. (2014). *From animals to anarchism: Open letter #3*. Leeds: Dysophia.

Webb, R. (2004). Animal liberation – By 'whatever means necessary'. In S. Best & A. J. Nocella (Eds.), *Terrorists or freedom fighters?: Reflections on the liberation of animals*. New York: Lantern Books.

Winsten, S. (1951). *Salt and his circle*. London: Hutchinson & Co.

3. Bringing Down the Animal Abuse Industry by Any Means Necessary: State-corporate-media Alliance and the Fear of Counter-cultural Intervention

Erika Cudworth and Richard J. White

Introduction

Any activist praxis intent on bringing down the animal abuse industry must continuously envision new and creative ways to understand, engage and subvert the hegemonic relations that normalize human consumption of the flesh and milk of other animals. Drawing attention toward the culture of carnism, a key cultural aspect of the animal-industrial complex (A-IC), the chapter explores the ways in which the "meat culture" might be contested. Successful cultural interventions, insofar as they reject state-corporate-media propaganda and threaten to collapse the violent speciesist worlds of animal production and consumption, are a truly terrifying prospect for those involved in the animal abuse industry. In this context, we encourage activists to creatively find ways to use laughtivism to expose, mock and ridicule A-IC, and its supporters, as a means of engaging a wider audience, and in doing so enable a radical politics of sight to further expose the violence and horrors rooted in (our) carnist culture.

The chapter is divided into five key sections. First, the animal industrial complex is addressed, paying particular attention toward how animal exploitation is tightly embedded in globalized corporate capitalism systems. This is followed by exploring the dominant culture of carnism and laying bare the multiple myths that underpin and perpetuate carnist belief systems. The third section focuses on how the A-IC responds violently to any action it deems threatening enough to undermine it. This, it will be shown, has manifest itself in many appalling ways, not least in the way in which animal rights and environmental activists have been effectively branded as domestic terrorists, and anti-terrorist legislation has been used to offer animal abuse industries greater legal protection. The central focus of the chapter considers how cultural interventions – through television and films, for example – have been important means of challenging carnist normalcy. Here, particular attention is made toward *Animals* (1981), *Cowspiracy* (2015) and *Carnage* (2017). The chapter concludes by reflecting on the importance of humor and satire, laughtivism, as a creative way of undermining and exposing the A-IC and educating and persuading more people to identify with the cause of animal liberation and compassionate vegan politics.

The Animal Industrial Complex

U.S. President Dwight Eisenhower's farewell address of 1957 warned of the influence of a "military-industrial complex" that was to be found "in every city, every State House, every office of the Federal Government" (quoted in Parry, 1969, p. 64). The US sociologist Charles Wright Mills predated Eisenhower, using the concept of the "military-industrial complex" in *The Power Elite* (1956). In this and *The Causes of World War Three*, Mills understood the key problematic of his age, the 1950s, to be the existential threat of the arms race and militarism, which he considered to be a structural feature of the post-war world: "part of the contemporary sensibility -- and a defining characteristic of our epoch" (Mills, 1958, p. 1). Mills understood the "drift and thrust" towards nuclear war to result from the structural imperatives of the military-industrial complex which binds the interests of certain large corporations with military and scientific hierarchies to form a complex of interwoven relations of interdependency (1958, p. 22). This military industrial system makes both militarism and war appear inevitable; it normalises and enables a situation of permanent war and preparation for war. Yet for Mills, this inevitability is socially constituted and perpetuated by the mass media, the political class, the business elite, academe and organised religion (1958, pp. 2, 6, 17–18).

This concept of an industrial complex has been applied to other areas of social life, such as entertainment industries (Christopherson & Storper, 1986), carceral systems – the "prison–industrial complex" (Davies, 1999) and the "pharmaceutical-industrial complex" (Abraham, 2010). As Richard Twine points out, these industrial complexes could capture elements of our relationships to non-human animals (Twine, 2012, pp. 14–15). We would agree with Twine however, that the idea of an animal-industrial complex is more useful.

This was first used by Barbara Noske (1989) who suggests by this concept the extent to which and the ways in which human-animals relations are industrialized and "embedded in the capitalist fabric" (1997[1989], p. 22). The A-IC involves all the interrelated industries of agriculture (breeding and raising, feedstuff production), meat and dairy product manufacture (slaughter and processing) and distribution and sale through which animals become food. The business of animal research is part of the complex, as are financial interests, governing institutions and hi-tech, pharma and the military.

Crucial to the complex is its political constitution. As Noske suggests, the systems of animal agriculture do not develop in response to public demand, but are embedded in networks of industrial capitalism (from research, investment and financing to those of production and consumption) and produced by transnational corporations, such as Unilever (1997: 23). She describes the complex as "ever expanding and self-perpetuating," meeting needs that Western consumers learn to perceive as "real" (1997, p. 38). Key to Noske's argument is that the mass exploitation of non-human animals through globalised industrial production of animal-based foods has been possible through corporate capitalist systems. Critical approaches to animal studies have also deployed a critique of capitalism in relation to animal oppression (Best, 2006; Nibert, 2002; Nibert 2017a, 2017b; Twine, 2010; White, 2017) and followed Noske's emphasis on intersectionality (Cudworth, 2011).

As Twine (2012) notes, links can be made between different industrial complexes – pharmaceutical, entertainment and carceral – when it comes to mapping different elements of human relations with non-human animals and the interdependence of the crop and vegetable industries with those around livestock and animal feed (Twine, 2012, p. 19). The pet food industry should also be considered a lucrative element of the A-IC. Pet foods have always been produced from the leftover parts of animals which are not to be used for human food such as bones, organs, ears, skin and so on. However, the industry expanded massively since the mid twentieth century such that by 2007, the pet food industry in the US alone had sales of $16.1 billion (Nestle, 2008, p. 42). Twine suggests that sociological approaches to understanding human-animal relations, particularly critical ones, may make good use of the A-IC as a way to understand forms and practices of domination through multiple scope and levels. Twine offers a clear definition of the A-IC as a partly opaque and multiple set of networks and relationships between the corporate (agricultural) sector, governments, and public and private science. With economic, cultural, social and affective dimensions it encompasses an extensive range of practices, technologies, images, identities and markets (Twine, 2012, p. 23).

Others have used this notion of the A-IC to tease out the ways in which the media operates to legitimate, institutionalise and reproduce the hegemonic relations of meat eating and dairy consumption (Fitzgerald & Taylor, 2014; also Morgan & Cole, 2011). This has come to be described as "meat culture" or a culture of "carnism." It is this cultural aspect of the A-IC that this chapter is particularly concerned with, and the ways in which in the current context, it might be contested.

A Culture of Carnism

As Melanie Joy (2010) points out, all cultures demarcate species that cannot be eaten and those which can (p. 13). A common Western response to the idea of eating dog is disgust, but what is of most significance, Joy challenges, is that most people do not experience disgust at the thought of eating the very small range of animals which Western cultures deems edible. We do not experience disgust because meat eating is an established social practice and normative in our culture. We believe it is legitimate – both ethical and appropriate – to eat animals such as cows, pigs and sheep and this constitutes a belief system Joy calls "carnism" (p. 29). The A-IC feeds into, supports and is legitimated by meat culture.

Carnist belief systems are predicated on a series of myths revolving around what Joy terms the three "N's" of justification: that eating meat is normal, natural and necessary. These ideas are so ingrained in our consciousness that we do not have to think about them – we have internalised them as truths (2010, p. 95–7). Professionals such as veterinarians, doctors and non-government organizations (NGOs) supporting corporate agribusiness represent institutionalised carnism and function as "emissaries for [carnist] myths" whilst the mass media "reinforce the carnist message of the way things are" (Joy, 2010, p. 100 & 105). Whilst conformity is culturally rewarded, deviance is punished and thus "vegetarians often find themselves having to defend their choices, explain their diet, and apologize for inconveniencing others" (Joy, 2010, p. 106). Joy makes the simple but important point that in a carnist society where meat eating is customary and traditional, its longevity as an established cultural practice makes it easier to justify and far more difficult to question. A second key form of justification is "naturalization." Practices such as meat eating are seen to be in line with the laws of nature and having a biological basis (2010, pp. 107–8). Third, and closely connected, is the belief that eating meat is necessary, particularly for health, but also for economic growth and stability (2010, pp. 109–13). Joy considers carnism to be a system whose beliefs we internalise, but considers this might be counteracted by (re) awakening empathy for animals and invigorating disgust for the meat offered on a plate.

However, we argue that Joy underestimates the ability of systemic social relations to reproduce themselves here. It is not enough to crack the carnist system and assume that once empathy and disgust are engendered, a moral compass in which all animal products are eschewed follows. Rather, the questions of boundary drawing are more complicated. Erica Fudge emphasises this re-inscribing of boundaries in terms of what species of animal are and are not eaten. For vegans, boundaries are clearest of all, and for vegetarians they are reasonably clear in that "beings with animate life" are "not to be eaten." It is meat eaters who live, she says, with boundary confusion, continually making decisions about "where the boundary between the edible and inedible exists" (Fudge, 2008, pp. 18–19). Both Joy and Fudge underestimate, however, how the boundaries are blurred even for some vegetarians and vegans.

As Erika Cudworth (2016) has found that for those who live with companion animals, the questions of "who" eats "what" mammals, birds and fishes, are problematic. This is particularly so for those who live with dogs (biologically classified as carnivores, but often seen as omnivores with a physical and undeniable carnivorous bias) and cats (classified as carnivores and often seen as "obligate carnivores"). Carnist categorisations might be shifted and disturbed by the practice of living with an animal companion, and also such categories find ways of reconfiguring in Cudworth's study. In interviews focusing on their lives with dogs, many people discussed the food they fed their dogs and often this also spilled over into talk of what they ate themselves. The majority of interviewees were carnists, but many of these placed restrictions on the range of animals they would eat and many were also concerned for the welfare of animals other than dogs. In this sense, they are dealing with the problematic boundaries of the animals we may and may not eat, and for many, this was troubling. Most interesting were the vegetarian and (lone) vegan dog owner(s) for whom one might imagine the carnist glass to have cracked. In every case, companion animals in the home were fed meat, a carnism by proxy perhaps. Although these interviewees resisted elements of meat culture in their eating, they seemed very much influenced by carnist normalcy when it came to feeding animal companions. This suggests that carnism re-inscribes itself in the ways in which veg(etari)ans living with dogs discuss the ambiguities, tensions and reconciliations between their belief systems and the practice of feeding meat to the dogs-of-their-heart.

There are certainly alternatives to meat-based diets for animal companions. In the UK, vegan veterinarian Andrew Knight has been a pioneering force, drawing together research on the health benefits of meat-free diets for dogs and cats and defending veg(etari)an diets for companion animals as at least as healthy, if not healthier (Knight, 2005, 2015). The website Vegepets promotes such diets, recommending suppliers, brands and diets for animal companions (see www.vegepets.com). However, this is a limited commercial presence in the UK. Key pet food manufacturers have rapidly expanding markets, demonstrating popular belief among "owners" of companion animals in the necessity of animal-based food. This belief is, of course, socially constituted, and its contestation minimized.

The ingredients of pet foods, their journey "from farm to bowl" and the animal testing involved with most large corporate enterprises are obscured by the packaging and advertising of pet foods. Rather, advertising campaigns specifically target positive relations of care and concern that human owners have for the cats and dogs they assume responsibility for feeding (Proctor & Gamble, 2014), thereby inscribing carnist norms. For example, consider the advertisement for Iams cat food in which the human voiceover of the cat "actor" declares, "I am not a vegetarian. These teeth were made for meat" (Iams, 2012). Given the obvious affection and love in relational ties between people and animal companions, this carnist culture of pet food advertising is pernicious in suggesting that those who care for animal companions are obligated to feed those they love, other, dead, animals. The culture of carnism then, inscribes who (or "what") is killable (Wolfe, 2013), who can be made to live and made to die, and for whom. We have, then, an embedded, lucrative A-IC legitimating its existence through a range of cultural tropes so powerful that even those who question some elements of the A-IC may be implicated in others. The challenge for those of us seeking to undermine and contest the domination of animals is sufficient and as we will see below, the A-IC resists attempts to undermine it.

Fear and Protest: Contesting the A-IC

The A-IC – just as Mills would have expected of the M-IC – takes to be a threat any action which might undermine the complex and lucrative links between different elements of industrial production both domestic and international, between the State and investors. In deploying the term the "Green Scare," activist and journalist Will Potter (2011) has described a disturbing rhetoric of terrorism through which animal rights and environmental activism was demonized in the United States post 9/11 and suggests that parallels might be drawn with the anti-communist "Red Scare" of the 1940s and 1950s. The term "eco-terrorism," often used in such political rhetoric and media coverage, was coined by Ron Arnold, founder of the so-called "wise-use movement" (1993, p. 25; see Smith, 2008). Arnold suggested that a new kind of environmentalism had emerged, using terrorists' tactics to undermine corporate profit, for example, in the case of protests against logging. Politically well-connected advocates such as Arnold have worked with corporate lobby groups pushing for the criminalization of such dissent in order to "defend animal capital" through sustained and pre-emptive approaches to repression (Sanbonmatsu, 2011, p. 26). John Sabonmatsu argues that animal exploitation is a leading source of value under capitalist relations and as such, the state will act to repress movements which threaten this. This use of terror as a framing device for protest is a technique of neoliberal governmentality (Ayres, 2004) and also has significant impact on activism.

For Steve Best (2004), the criminalization of activists as domestic terrorists constitutes a "war" on animal liberation (also Black & Black, 2004). Colin Salter (2011) suggests that the labelling of activism as terrorism does not separate good (legal) from bad (illegal) activity, but rather sets up shifting boundaries in which any critical activity may be seen as causing terror. Thus, critical scholars of human-animal relations in academia might be targeted (Salter, 2011, p. 231) or material on websites might be held to in itself constitute a terrorist threat (Potter, 2011, p. 677). To illustrate, in the long running protest against vivisection in the laboratories of Huntingdon Life Sciences (HLS) in the UK and the US, the anti-vivisection group Stop Huntingdon Animal Cruelty (SHAC) used "Wall Street level knowledge of how corporations operate" to undermine HLS by targeting their financial backers (Potter, 2011, p. 677) in addition to the usual tactics of demonstration, symbolic protest and appeals to public opinion.

Prior to 9/11, animal rights "terrorism" was seen as a most significant threat by the FBI in the US and Special Branch and MI5 in the UK. In the UK, for example, in 1986 the Special Branch had set up a police intelligence gathering unit, the Animal Rights National Index (ARNI), but its task was restricted to collating information and advising regional police forces. After its remit was extended, Anti-Terrorist Branch officers became involved in animal rights policing for the first time in 1991 (UAR, 2018). In 2005, U.K. Trade and Industry Secretary Patricia Hewitt announced a legal amendment which was to make it a criminal offence to cause economic damage through organised campaigns of intimidation, and it became illegal to disrupt the lawful functioning of a business. The Serious Organised Crime and Police Act, which came into force in July 2005, gave industries conducting research using animals further protections. While the full blown use of anti-terrorism legislation has been limited (Monaghan, 2013), evidence has recently come to light in the news media that undercover operations tracked animal liberation

activists, often with rather unexpected fall out (Casciani, 2014). The UK
Government's controversial "Prevent" strategy has led to some discussion of
the relative threat of Islamists as compared to animal rights radicalisation at
British Universities (Garahan, 2011; H.M. Government, 2011, p. 50). The
ability of the A-IC to secure itself through a nexus of supportive media cover-
age, corporate lobbying and policy responses (such as the Animal Enterprise
Terrorism Act of 1992 in the US) meant that advocates for the A-IC, such as
Ron Arnold in the 1980s, were effective.

For Salter (2011), the pernicious impact of the Green Scare has been
self-censorship and self-regulation by activists and advocates campaigning to
undermine the oppression of non-human animals. Such constructions of dissent are not only recent incarnations of neo-liberal governmentality (Rose,
1999) but also exemplify the kind of repressive tolerance practised in liberal
democracies that Herbert Marcuse identified in the 1950s and 1960s, and of
which Mills was very much aware (see Khan, 2006). In such a context, the
"war" against animal liberation is also importantly fought against animal
abuse through undermining anthroparchal culture (Cudworth, 2011). The
second half of this chapter considers how effective cultural interventions of
animal advocacy have been, focussing in particular on the impact of film.

Counter-Cultural Intervention: From the Politics of Sight to Laughtivism

Culture wars have long been fought in the struggle to undermine the domination of non-human animals and secure change. Documentaries on television
and in film, dramatised real life accounts and fictional narratives, have carried
messages of criticism and demands for change, as in the *Born Free* (Hill,
Jaffe, & Radin, 1966) film of the 1960s or *Blackfish* in the 2000s. *Blackfish*
(Cowperthwaite & Oteya, 2013) has been directly linked to Sea Worlds'
decision to stop breeding captive orcas and having them perform (Boomey,
2016). Such cultural interventions have clearly had an impact on mainstream
commercial entertainment, such as in the case of *Free Willy* (Wincer, Shulder
Donner, & Law Tugend, 1993) or the second *Finding Nemo* film *Finding
Dory* (Stanton & Collins, 2016). Such cultural phenomena may have greater
ease of traction in terms of their acceptance, however, than those depicting
creatures that are domesticate and that are to be eaten. The ways in which
McDonald's attempted and failed to use merchandise capitalising on the success of the film *Babe* (Noonan & Kennedy, 1995) is a case in point. The film
was popular with children but did represent a (partial) challenge to carnist
normalcy in the figure of Ferdinand the duck who made very clear what the

function of farming was and that the fate of animals like himself, and Babe the pig, was to become meat. Thus to use animal toy tie-ins to sell meat products was, in this case, not successful (see Cole & Morgan, 2011).

The Aardman animation *Chicken Run* (Lord & Park, 2000) caused less of a stir in its UK home base, although arguably, the questions it raised about the lives and deaths of laying hens were poignant and clear: oppressed and facing eventual certain death, chickens on farms are incarcerated before being slaughtered and made into pies. Rocky the rooster and Ginger the chicken decide to rebel against the farm's owners ("Mrs. Tweedy, the chickens are revolting!"). They lead their fellow chickens in a great escape to a paradise in which eggs hatch and chickens are raised to adulthood and beyond! We wait in anticipation to see how much the narrative may have shifted in the last decade and a half in the forthcoming sequel (BBC, 2017).

What the above films illustrate is the use of "real" cases and pure fiction, or a combination of the two, both to entertain the viewer and to raise questions about the role and status of animals in human dominant society. This section will consider in more detail, three examples of a kind of documentary film that is particularly explicit in attempting to intervene in anthroparchal culture (Cudworth, 2011) in a politicized and directly contestationary way. These films are *Animals* (Alaux & Schonfeld, 1981), *Cowspiracy* (Anderson, Khun, & DiCaprio, 2015), and *Carnage* (Amstell & O'Connor, 2017). While all three firms have similar elements, the messages they deliver are differently cast in terms of method. All use satire to different degrees and two use humour, but only one, *Carnage* can be seen as an example of laughtivism.

In 1981, in the launch week of new terrestrial station Channel 4, the *Animals* film was screened on British television. At the time, it contained radical and shocking material for a mass audience as it surveyed how and why modern societies exploit animals in factory farming, as pets, for entertainment, in scientific and military research, in hunting mammals such as foxes with dogs (which was then legal in the UK) and so on. It also profiled the international animal rights movement. The film incorporated secret government footage and scenes that had never been filmed or shown before. As a documentary, the film was also noteworthy for its ground-breaking ironic style, integrating diverse found footage including cartoons, newsreels, advertisements, and government propaganda films, mingled with vox pops alongside scenes of illegal animal liberation raids and interviews with campaigners. This film set a new benchmark for film media which attempted to undermine the tropes of anthroparchal normalcy.

The impact on some of its audience from 1981 to the present can be seen from the comments on the Amazon page selling the DVD. As Anat

Pick (2017) comments, this film "lays bare" the scope of human atrocities against animals. It enacts a "politics of sight" which exposes hidden realities. While it uses irony in order to deliver its message, this is a very challenging film to watch not because of the graphic images of violence and abuse towards animals, but because there are few breaks in such imagery – there is a relentless quality to the film. Similar online comments can be found to describe *Earthlings* (2005), a documentary very similar in content and style to *Animals* and described by viewers as overwhelming and depressing. It was this film that "upset" British comedian and comedy writer Simon Amstell into veganism, however:

> It was so upsetting that whenever I recommended it to anyone, when they asked "why are you vegan?" I said "this film *Earthlings*, you must watch it", and they would say "I will not watch it" (in Wallis, 2017).

This made Amstell question the effectiveness of an unmediated politics of sight which presents atrocity after atrocity as a means of "upsetting" people into veganism. And as we will see below, it led him to use comedy in his own film.

The politics of sight is the key to the success of a more recent intervention, *Cowspiracy* (2015), a documentary produced and directed by Kip Andersen and Keegan Kuhn, which explores the global impact of the A-IC, specifically animal agriculture, on the environment. The film is different to *Animals* and *Earthlings* in using a narrative device and a mockumentary style. The opening scene introduces the main narrative character Kip, inspired by Al Gore's film *An Inconvenient Truth*, to wake up to the threat of climate change. In embracing environmentalism, Kip cycled everywhere, recycled his trash and turned off light switches. He then had a moment of enlightenment when a post from a friend referencing the UN *Livestock's Long Shadow* report suggested that animal agriculture is a key cause of climate change. Kip and fellow filmmaker Keegan then proceed to take us along on his sometimes frustrating, sometimes amusing investigative journey exploring the ways in which meat production exploits land, water and other natural resources, undermines biodiversity, and contributes both to climate change and unhealthy human diets.

Through statistics and creative animated infographics peppered along its feature-length, the constant focus of the film is animal agriculture rather than any other sites of the domination, exploitation and abuse of animals. The film argues that

> Animal agriculture is the leading cause of deforestation, water consumption and pollution, is responsible for more greenhouse gases than the transportation

industry, and is a primary driver of rainforest destruction, species extinction, habitat loss, topsoil erosion, ocean "dead zones," and virtually every other environmental ill. Yet it goes on, almost entirely unchallenged.

The film also considers the policies of particular environmental organisations including Greenpeace, the Sierra Club and the Rainforest Action Network and the ways in which these organisations fail to intervene to mitigate the environmental degradation caused by eating animals. Andersen contacts one environmental organisation after another, hoping to tackle the issue of why animal agriculture is such a taboo subject for them and is repeatedly given evasive answers to questions and denied interviews.

Since its release, the film claims to have triggered major behavioural change among young adults. Both the film's Facebook page and the video-sharing site Vimeo carry comments from around the world, with a good number declaring an instant conversion to veganism (*New Internationalist*, 2015). There are similarities and differences to the model we saw in *Animals*. The latter is relentless in depicting the violence and abuse animals suffer at human hands, and the systematic quality of this violence. In contrast, *Cowspiracy* is a mockumentary and uses some humour – for example the evasive behaviour of politicians, activists and corporate executives is funny – while splicing in scenes of violence as animals are caught on film being killed. This film attempts to draw its audience along in part by entertaining them, in addition to enacting a politics of sight. This appears to have contributed to the popularity of *Cowspiracy* in attracting an audience.

Of course, there were critics. While the film was popular and won various awards, its factual claims were contested, in particular the film's claim that 51% of global greenhouse gases are caused by animal agriculture. In responding to this criticism, Khun (2015) claims this is evading the key intention of the film which "was to raise awareness of the single most destructive industry facing the planet today: animal agriculture." *Cowspiracy*'s Indiegogo pitch document states with missionary zeal that "we aren't just creating a movie, we are creating a movement" (*New Internationalist*, 2015). And it was not only young people who responded to this new movement. Mainstream media coverage of the film was less hostile than might have been expected, with *The Guardian* and *The Independent* newspapers in the UK quick to publicise different scientific responses which debated the "true" impact of the A-IC on climate change and other environmental issues.

Cowspiracy is certainly less relentless than *Animals*, and there are moments of light relief. (While it is easier to watch, however, there is still an element of instruction – we are being told how to act.) Similarly, the key attraction of films aimed mainly but not exclusively at children, such as *Chicken Run* or

Babe, is that they are entertaining and humorous, but they also raise some difficult questions about the role of animals without engendering bite-back from the A-IC in the way that *Cowspiracy* did. This brings us to the unique film *Carnage* and the core question: when the situation of all kinds of animals is so desperate, is it inappropriate to challenge anthroparchy (Cudworth, 2011) through what has been called "laughtivism"?

The association of carnivalesque politics with social movements has a well- established history (Hart & Bos, 2007; Sørensen, 2017). In working to undermine the Slobodan Milošević regime in Serbia, Srdja Popovic coined the term "laughtivism." He argues that the use of humour and satire in political protests is a powerful way to attract members to a social movement and also undermine the ability of the police to discipline protestors (Popovic, 2015; Popovic & Jaksci, 2013). For Mikhail Bakhtin (1984), laughter is critical in his notion of carnivalesque politics because it represents a vital counter to the serious, ordered official world. The carnivalesque style of activism emphasises the deconstruction of relations, including those between activists and police, to create an uncontrollable space, unfamiliar to both but particularly disorientating for state power (Karatzogianni & Robinson, 2009). Drawing attention to the profound, radical potential that humour has, Kutz-Flamenbaum argues that:

> ... humor is a core communicative strategy used to build affiliative ties, expand groups, strengthen communities, and attempt to educate, entertain, and persuade. In its ability to disarm and entertain, humor holds profound potential for changing people's minds and promoting social change. As novelist George Orwell (1968) is often quoted as saying, "Every joke is a tiny revolution" and it has the merit too of making people laugh. (2014, p. 294)

Simon Amstell is a controversial comedian asked by the BBC if he might produce something both "peculiar" and "daring" (Ewans, 2017). Amstell came up with *Carnage* (2017), of which he is writer and director. He claims to be a "clown" rather than an activist, yet his film, unlike *Cowspiracy*, can be read as a strong example of laughtivism. *Carnage* appears to be similar in its mockumentary format but is really very different – the use of satire here is crucial to the film and making people laugh is the medium of the vegan message. *Carnage* has been described by Amstell and interviewer and film commentator Mark Kermode, as a "vegan science fiction film" (BFI, 2017). This is not science fiction, however, but speculative fiction. The world *Carnage* imagines is very much embedded in our own and emergent from it. The film takes us on a vegan mock history of Britain from 1944 to 2067 when veganism is the norm and carnism is banned. He situates his film in the future from where he might critique things he currently finds appalling. Thus, *Carnage* looks back on meat-eating as "a time," says Amstell, the narrator, "before we realised we had to stop eating each other."

The film opens with ethereal, kindly, tactile young people expressing their disbelief at how people could have ever killed and eaten animals: "Why would anyone eat a baby? Just a little baby, a little baby lamb?" The mockumentary narrative is one of reconciliation – enabling a young generation of vegans in 2067 to understand why their parents, and particularly their grandparents, ate animals. By the end of the film, abattoirs become museums in the style of Holocaust memorials. There is no word for vegan, as one of Amstell's activists declares in a television interview: "We're not vegan. They're carnists." The last milk chocolate egg is preserved in a museum as a "chilling reminder of a culture which once stole a cow's milk and moulded it into a chicken's egg."

This film uses laugh-out-loud humour to make some hard-hitting points. Dr. Yasmine Vondenburgen, a terribly sincere psychotherapist, holds support sessions for former carnists to assuage their guilt about their meat-eating pasts. Carnists need to be treated with compassion, says Vondenburgen, because former carnists like herself "couldn't have known we were active participants in a slave trade because the language of the time suggested we were just eating our dinner." The film's "story of how meat became people" begins in 1944, with the establishment of the Vegan Society, and rationing of meat due to war. After rationing, which ends in 1954, cultural promotion of vegetables ends and we see the first British celebrity, Chef Fanny Cradock, promoting carnism on television. In the 1970s and 1980s, US food companies use toys (animal toys or meat toys) to promote carnist fast food, accompanied by the well-known figures of "the Clown, the Captain and the King all masterfully diverting the public's attention from this," says Amstell; "this" being footage of animals in factory farms and slaughterhouses. The film pans through decades of adverts, TV shows and cultural artefacts, which – in the context of the new vegan world of 2067 – are made to look very strange.

Standout moments involve current celebrity chefs who have promoted so-called ethical meat, such as Gordon Ramsay and Hugh Fearnley-Wittingstall, who help allay the concerns of middle class people that "they could be eating the same unethical food as poor people" and "showed them how they could eat free-range animals." Jamie Oliver's campaign against cheap processed meat in school canteens is presented as an effort to replace "mashed up flesh with non-mashed up flesh." In a particularly arresting use of TV cookery footage, a smiling and sensuous Nigella Lawson prepares a chicken, commenting on how much she admires and respects the bird before casually smashing the carcass's' rib cage with her hands by putting all her weight down onto the body. The film explores Amstell's imagined cultural and economic arena of struggle, where the vegan movement grows in Britain and manages to overthrow a country that's always seen to adore meat. There is resistance to the building vegan revolution, and the comedy highlight here comes in the form of a furious middle-class white man who feels unsettled in a changing world and livestreams himself ranting and going into vegan cafes and mocking the customers with: "Does this make you interesting? Do you eat this food because you think you don't look smug enough?"

Here we find one of the most important elements of this film, for vegans are satirised heavily too. We find ourselves laughing out loud when a well-known British actress, playing the part of a committed feminist vegan academic, describes the trauma of not being able to bury a key activist because he had been murdered and eaten by the Great British Meat League. We are shown rare clips of vegans in the media from the 1970s which are toe-curlingly embarrassing and even by the 1990s "the vegans were still ridiculous and rarely allowed on television." In the 2000s, Paul McCartney's "meat free Monday" campaign is about as offensive as "ethnic-cleansing-free Tuesday," and a former PETA activist recalls "pretending to die a lot and being ignored," while in the 2020s vegan performance art is an object of ridicule. In reflecting on this element of the film, Amstell says that enabling meat eating viewers to laugh along *with* vegans and *at* vegans was essential to the film as an effective piece of entertainment with a vegan viewpoint. He says in reference to its script: "If at any point *Carnage* became on paper preachy or annoying, we made sure something really funny was really near to that bit so people would be laughing rather than feeling judged. It is quite a compassionate film" (in Ewans, 2017).

On the BBC page where the film is to be found, there now are answers to "ten top questions raised by the film," including whether meat production and consumption causes climate change, the origin of the term vegan, whether animals could be given the same rights as humans and whether we "could really turn vegan by 2067" (BBC, 2018). Amstell definitely intended this film to make a political intervention despite his denial about himself as an activist. In contrast, we do think he is a laughtivist activist. His aim was to make something that was watchable and which would make people laugh "so that the message could be put across in a way that didn't traumatise people" (in Wallis, 2017); he considered that this was also key to keeping non-vegans engaged with the content because

> The problem with everything vegan you ever hear is that [...] there's a superiority to it, so the intention was to make something kind of self-deprecating and funny enough that you didn't mind when a new bit of information was

presented. You wouldn't mind too much when we told you that male chicks get gassed or shredded.

This does appear to have been an effective strategy, for in a review of *Carnage* in *The Independent* newspaper, Max Benwall (2017) argues that

> Carnage is an almost perfect example of how to push a worthwhile message without being preachy. And in what must be a world-first for vegan activism, it even takes the piss out of vegans. [...] Carnage works because it's very funny, entertaining, but also shows how society can be made to change its mind. It's not about shaming anyone, or bombarding them with stats. Instead, the film asks a simple question: how will we look back on our treatment of animals in 50 years?

Alex Crocker (2017) notes, "For every serious point, there is a joke, and for every joke you will come away with a feeling that it raised a very good point." The overall effect, says Crocker, "is that it presents veganism in such a way you often don't even notice it's being done," and that does seem to have disturbed some of his own "meaty practices" (Arcari, 2018). The film's sub-title is "swallowing the past," and what Amstell is doing is to use humour to enable possibly antagonistic viewers to swallow his vegan message.

In revealing the A-IC, in both exposing and laughing at its defenders and exposing them to ridicule, we can break into the ideological reproduction of carnist culture. The message of cultural interventions is that we need both civil action in the form of protest and in building an engaging, inclusive and compassionate vegan politics. The dominant meaty practices are certainly based on a materiality of carnage, but as Amstell's film suggests, a politics of sight that makes arguments through making people laugh might engage a wider audience. Laughtivism then, we think, may be an enabler of a radical politics of sight.

References

Abraham, J. (2010). Pharmaceuticalisation of society in context: Theoretical, empirical and health dimensions. *Sociology, 44*(4), 603–622.

Alaux, M., & Schonfeld, V. (Directors) and Beyond the Frame (Producer) (1981). *Animals* [Motion picture] UK: Beyond the Frame/Slik Pix.

Amstell, S. (Director), Amstell, S., & O'Connor, D. (Producers) (2017). *Carnage* [Motion picture] BBC, London, UK. On-line, retrieved from: https://www.daily-motion.com/video/x5txizo

Anderson, K., Khun, K. (Producers), & DiCaprio, L. (Director) (2015). *Cowspiracy*. Los Angeles, U.S.: Netflix.

Arcari, P. (2018). *Making Sense of 'Food' Animals: A critical exploration of the persistence of 'meat'*, unpublished PhD thesis, RMIT University, Melbourne, Australia.

Arnold, R. (1993). *Ecology wars: Environmentalism as if people mattered*. Washington: Merril Press.

Ayres, J. M. (2004). Framing collective action against neoliberalism. *Journal of World Systems Research, 10* (1 Special Issue: Global Social Movements Before and After 9–11), 11–34.

Bakhtin, M. (1984). *Rabelais and his World*. Bloomington: Midland Books, Indiana University Press.

BBC (2017). Chicken Run 2: Sequel confirmed after 18-year wait, 27 April https://www.bbc.co.uk/news/uk-43922140. Accessed 15th June 2018.

BBC (British Broadcasting Corporation) (2018). Carnage: The facts. Retrieved from http://www.bbc.co.uk/programmes/articles/VN3BnwnWKCytkfzhxL1BB4/carnage-the-facts. Accessed 23rd June 2018.

Benwall, M. (2017). Carnage, review: Simon Amstell has made the world's first vegan comedy that's actually funny. Retrieved from https://www.independent.co.uk/arts-entertainment/tv/carnage-review-bbc-iplayer-simon-amstell-vegan-comedy-actually-funny-a7636871.html. Accessed 23rd June 2018.

Best, S. (2004). 'It's war! The escalating battle between activists and the corporate-state complex'. In S. Best & A. J. Nocella (Eds.), *Terrorists or freedom fighters: Reflections on the liberation of animals*. New York, NY: Lantern Books.

Best, S. (2006). Rethinking revolution: Animal liberation, human liberation and the future of the left. *The International Journal of Inclusive Democracy, 2*(3), 1–24.

BFI (2017). Simon Amstell on his vegan sci-fi Carnage, https://www.youtube.com/watch?v=DMcli9vhM2I. Accessed 30th August 2018.

Black, J., & Black, J. (2004). The rhetorical "terrorist": Implications of the USA patriot act on animal liberation. In S. Best & A. J. Nocella (Eds.), *Terrorists or freedom fighters: Reflections on the liberation of animals* (pp. 300–339). New York: Lantern Books.

Boomey, J. (2016). SeaWorld to phase out killer whale shows, captivity, *USA Today* 17th March 2016. Retrieved from https://eu.usatoday.com/story/money/2016/03/17/seaworld-orcas-killer-whales/81900498/. Accessed 19th June 2018.

Casciani, D. (2014). The undercover cop, his lover, and their son *BBC News Magazine*. Retrieved from https://www.bbc.co.uk/news/magazine-29743857. Accessed 21st June 2018.

Christopherson, S., & Storper, M. (1986). The city as studio; the world as back lot: The impact of vertical disintegration on the location of the motion picture industry. *Environment and Planning D: Society and Space, 4*(3), 305–320.

Cowperthwaite, G. (Director) and Cowperthwaite, G., & Oteya, M. V. (Producers) (2013). *Blackfish* [Motion picture] U.S.: CNN Films.

Crocker, A. (2017). A meat eater's reaction to vegan mockumentary Carnage. Retrieved from https://www.livekindly.co/vegan-mockumentary-carnage/. Accessed 23rd June 2018.

Cudworth, E. (2011). *Social lives with other animals: Tales of sex, death and love*. Basingstoke: Palgrave.

Cudworth, E. (2016). On ambivalence and resistance: Carnism and diet in multispecies households. In A. Potts (Ed.), *Critical perspectives on meat culture*. Leiden: Brill.

Davies, A. (1999). *The prison-industrial complex*. Chico, CA: AK Press.

Ewans, H. (2017). Simon Amstell On His New Vegan Mockumentary, "Carnage", *Vice*, 13th March 2017, retrieved from https://www.vice.com/en_uk/article/vvj7k3/simon-amstell-on-his-new-vegan-mockumentary-carnage. Accessed 21st June 2018.

Fitzgerald, A. J. & Taylor, N. (2014). The cultural hegemony of meat and the animal industrial complex. In N. Taylor &R. Twine (Eds.), *The rise of critical animal studies: From the margins to the centre* (pp. 165–182). London: Routledge.

Fudge, E. (2008). *Pets*. Stocksfield: Acumen.

Garahan, D. (2011). Animal rights extremists 'more of a problem than Islamists', *Daily Telegraph*, 18th February 2011. https://www.telegraph.co.uk/news/uknews/terrorism-in-the-uk/8333680/Animal-rights-extremists-more-of-a-problem-than-Islamists.html

Hart, M., & Bos, S. (Eds.). (2007). Humour and social protest. *International Review of Social History*, Supplement 15. Cambridge: Cambridge University Press.

Hill, J. (Director), Jaffe, S., & Radin, P. (Producers) (1966). *Born Free* [Motion picture] U.K.: Open Road films/Colombia Pictures.

H.M. Government (2011). Prevent Strategy, Cm8092, HMSO retrieved from https://assets.publishing.service.gov.uk/government/uploads/system/uploads/attachment_data/file/97976/prevent-strategy-review.pdf. Accessed 19th June 2018.

Iams. (2012). These teeth were made for meat. Retrieved from http://www.youtube.com/watch?v=rT3Ub2Ht_Z0 (advertisement uploaded by Iams 24 August, 2012). Accessed July 10th 2014.

Joy, M. (2010). *Why we love dogs, eat pigs and wear cows: An introduction to carnism*. San Francisco, CA: Conari Press.

Kahn, R. (2006). Radical ecology, repressive tolerance, and zoöcide. In S. Best & A. J. Nocella (Eds.), *Igniting a revolution: Voices in defense of the earth*. Oakland, CA: AK Press.

Karatzogianni, A., & Robinson, A. (2009). *Power, resistance and conflict in the contemporary world: Social movements, networks and hierarchies*. London: Routledge.

Khun, K. (2015). Response to criticism of Cowspiracy facts. Retrieved from http://www.cowspiracy.com/blog/2015/11/23/response-to-criticism-of-cowspiracy-facts. Accessed 19th June 2018.

Knight, A. (2005). In defense of vegetarian cat food. *Journal of the American Veterinary Association, 226*(4), 512–513.

Knight, A. (2015). Can cats and dogs go vegetarian? http://www.andrewknight.info/presentations/vegetarian_pets.html. Accessed 26th October 2015.

Kutz-Flamenbaum, R. V. (2014). Humor and social movements. *Sociology Compass, 8*(3), 294–304.

Lord, P., & Park, N. (Directors), Aardman Animations (Producers) (2000). *Chicken run* [Motion picture]. London, UK: Dreamworks.

Mills, C. W. (1956). *The power elite*. New York, NY: Oxford University Press.

Mills, C. W. (1958). *The causes of world war three*. New York, NY: Simon and Schuster.

Monaghan, R. (2013). Not quite terrorism: Animal rights extremism in the United Kingdom. *Studies in Conflict and Terrorism, 36*(11), 933–951.

Monson, S. (Director and Producer) (2005). *Earthlings*. U.S.: Nation Earth.

Morgan, K., & Cole, M. (2011). The discursive representation of non-human animals in a culture of denial. In B. Cater & N. Charles (Eds.), *Human and other animals: Critical perspectives*. London: Palgrave Macmillan.

Nestle, M. (2008). *Pet food politics: The Chihuahua in the coalmine*. London: University of California Press.

New Internationalist. (2015). Beware Cowspiracy – and the spread of the vegan virus. Retrieved from https://newint.org/blog/2015/09/24/cowspiracy-documentary-vegan. Accessed 21st June 2018.

Nibert, D. (2002). *Animal rights/Human rights: Entanglements of oppression and liberation*. Lanham, Maryland: Rowman and Littlefield.

Nibert, D. (Ed.). (2017a). *Animal oppression and capitalism. Volume one: The oppression of nonhuman animals as sources of food*. Colarado: Praeger Press.

Nibert, D. (Ed.). (2017b). *Animal oppression and capitalism. Volume two: The oppressive and destructive role of capitalism*. Colarado: Praeger Press.

Noonan, C. (Director) and Kennedy Millar (Producer) (1995). *Babe* [Motion picture] New South Wales, Australia: Universal Pictures.

Noske, B. (1997 [1989]). *Beyond boundaries: Humans and animals* (Revised edition). Montreal: Black Rose Books.

Parry, G. (1969). *Political elites*. London: George Allen and Unwin.

Pick, A. (2017). Animal rights films, organized violence and the politics of sight. In C. Molloy & Y. Tzioumakis (Eds.), *The Routledge companion to cinema and politics*. Abingdon, Oxford: Routledge.

Popovic, S. (2015). *Blueprint for revolution: How to use rice pudding, Lego men, and other nonviolent techniques to Galvanize communities, overthrow dictators, or simply change the world*. New York, NY: Spiegal & Grau/Random house.

Popovic, S., & Jaksci, M. (2013). Why dictators don't like jokes, *Foreign Policy*. Retrieved from https://foreignpolicy.com/2013/04/05/why-dictators-dont-like-jokes/. Accessed 23rd June 2018.

Potter, W. (2011). *Green is the New Red: An insider's account of a social movement under siege*. San Francisco: City Lights Books.

Proctor & Gamble (2012). New campaign inspired by real stories from pet owners. Retrieved from http://news.pg.com/press-release/pg-corporate-announcements/iams-launches-new-campaign-inspired-real-stories-showcase-e#sthash.FH2P62g0.dpuf. Accessed 8th July 2014.

Rose, N. (1999). *Powers of freedom: Reframing political thought.* Cambridge: Cambridge University Press.

Salter, C. (2011). Activism as terrorism: The green scare, radical environmentalism and governmentality. *Anarchist Developments in Cultural Studies, 1*(2), 11–238.

Sanbonmatsu, J. (2011). Introduction. In J. Sanbonmatsu (Ed.), *Critical theory and animal liberation.* Lanham, MA: Rowman & Littlefield.

Smith, R. K. (2008). "Ecoterrorism"?: A critical analysis of the vilification of radical environmental activists as terrorists. *Environmental Law, 38,* 537–576.

Sørensen, M. J. (2017). Laughing on the way to social change: Humour and nonviolent action theory. *Peace & Change, 42*(1), 128–156.

Stanton, A. (Director) & Collins, L. (Producer) (2016). *Finding Dory* [Motion picture] U.S.: Walt Disney Pictures/Pixar Animation, U.S.

Twine, R. (2010). *Animals as biotechnology: Animals, ethics and critical animal studies.* London: Earthscan.

Twine, R. (2012). Revealing the "Animal-Industrial complex" – A concept and method for critical animal studies. *Journal for Critical Animal Studies, 10*(1), 12–39.

UAR (Understanding Animal Research) (2018). Outlawing animal rights extremism. Retrieved from http://www.understandinganimalresearch.org.uk/policy/animal-rights-extremism/outlawing-animal-rights-extremism/. Accessed 20th June 2018.

Wallis, L. (2017). Roving reporter Louise Wallis attends the press screening of 'Carnage', Simon Amstell's Vegan comedy film, *Vegan Life.* Retrieved from https://www.veganlifemag.com/simon-amstell-carnage-film/. Accessed 31st August 2018.

White, R. J. (2017). Rising to the challenge of capitalism and the commodification of animals: Post-capitalism, anarchist economies and vegan praxis. In D. Nibert (Ed.), *Animal oppression and capitalism.. Volume two: The oppressive and destructive role of capitalism.* Colorado: Praeger Press.

Wincer, S. (Director) & Shulder Donner, L., Law Tugend, J. (Producers) (1993). *Free Willy* [Motion Picture] U.S.: Le Studio Canal and Regency Enterprises, Warner Bros.

Wolfe, C. (2013). *Before the law: Human and other animals in biopolitical frame.* Chicago and London: Chicago University Press.

4. *Radicalizing Animal Theology: Moving toward a Revolutionary Praxis*

KYLE RAMSEY-SUMNER AND PIPER RAMSEY-SUMNER

Following on the heels of other liberation theologies, animal theologians have developed a theological response to the overwhelming number of non-human animals that suffer at the hands of humans throughout the world. Liberation theology is rooted in God's preferential option for the oppressed, meaning that God speaks through and for the poor and marginalized. This theology is rooted in praxis and is wholly concerned with social justice and liberation for all. It provides a framework upon which animal theologians can explore new ways of interacting with the non-human world. In this chapter, we argue that while animal theology has proven itself useful in opening up dialog around how people of faith might navigate human/non-human relationships and has significantly challenged the normalization of the use and abuse of non-human animals, this dialog has proven itself to be a double-edged sword.

While focusing on the concept that if one can change the way people think about animals, then they will change the way they treat animals, animal theologians have failed to significantly challenge the systemic nature of animal oppression. As a consequence of this oversight, they have found themselves in parallel with the contemporary animal rights movement in that their resistance to animal oppression can largely be summed up in their desire for vegan education and an overwhelmingly misguided trust in the capitalist system. In this chapter, as an attempt to push animal theology in a new direction that significantly challenges animal oppression at its roots, we point towards radical faith-based resistance movements as a source of reflection on what a radical animal theology might look like. This approach is not satisfied with reforming systems of oppression but instead seeks out new ways of being in the world that are committed to ending all forms of oppression, both human and non-human, by striking at the root of the problem.

What We Mean By "Radicalizing Animal Theology"

The word "radical" can mean many things to many people. When brought up in a conversation about theology, religion, and religious practice, the term can quickly become synonymous with religious extremism, bigotry, and fundamentalism. In an attempt to avoid confusion as to what we mean when we talk about "radicalizing animal theology," we must clarify what we mean when we use this powerful phrase. Like many others who have written extensively on the subject before us, we define as "radical" any group or individual that actively seeks out the root causes of a given problem rather than seeking to reform them through a system of already established boundaries.

For us, like the theologian Dorothee Soelle (1999), to become more "radical" has both a political and a theological dimension (pg. 47). The theologian must recognize that the theological and the political spheres are not somehow separated, but are always already informing one another. Therefore, to become more radical, politically speaking, necessarily demands one become more radical theologically. In other words, when one begins to recognize that the problems of animal exploitation are in fact a direct result of blind obedience to a system of hierarchy and domination, theologians are to reflect on the ways in which the Christian tradition has been complicit and participatory within these very systems and explore new ways to move forward. Likewise, when theologians begin to unearth and wrestle with deep-rooted problems of speciesism within the Christian tradition, their politics must begin to shift accordingly.

We anticipate that some animal theologians will inevitably respond to this claim by suggesting that this is indeed what they are doing in their work. That by recognizing the need to minimize animal suffering in the world, they have shifted their politics in such a way as to promote policy reforms, to educate the public on the necessity of a vegan diet, and to create theological and societal changes toward non-human animals. This oversimplified response to the problems of animal suffering, however, undermines the scholarship of theologians and Christian ethicists doing ethics from marginalized perspectives. Liberation theologians of marginalized communities have for decades insisted that those in positions of power and privilege must listen to and be transformed by the analysis constructed out of the lived experiences of the oppressed. While animal theologians have often argued that they are constructing a theology from the margins by taking the experience of non-human animals into account, they have largely failed to address the underlying oppressive power dynamics at play within their own critiques and worldviews. Animal theologians must listen to other theologians and ethicists who construct their work from marginalized perspectives and warn of the influence of Eurocentric Christian ethics and the oppressive nature of the systems that it preserves.

If a radical animal theology is to take seriously the idea of striking at the roots of animal oppression, then it must also loosen its grip on its commitment to reform political and economic institutions and policies via the established order. For if we take seriously the analysis put forward by communities of color and other marginalized communities, then we must recognize that animal oppression is not simply a result of poor consumer habits but is a direct result of well-established modes of thinking that are entrenched in our society. Thus, the problem of animal suffering is not something that can be fixed with a simple shift in values or practices, but requires deeper, revolutionary change. For the radical animal theologian, this means that writing letters to a congressperson or other powerbroker—or even acts of civil disobedience that are intended to appeal to power—are not viable means to animal liberation, as they serve to maintain and preserve the power dynamics that are at the root of oppressive behavior towards both humans and non-human animals.

Rather than seeking to reform oppressive institutions through voting, lobbying, creating laws and regulations, or gaining political leverage, radical animal theologians look to address the problems of animal exploitation through direct action. Unlike other approaches that seek to reform political and economic systems by appealing to the powers that be, direct action seeks to abolish those systems of power by building a new society within the shell of the old. As David Graeber (2009) notes, "Direct action is the insistence, when faced with structures of unjust authority, on acting as if one is already free. One does not solicit the state. One does not even necessarily make a grand gesture of defiance. Insofar as one is capable, one proceeds as if the state does not exist" (pg. 203). One takes direct action, whether that be liberating animals from a factory farm, sabotaging the progress of deforestation, or physically stopping a pipeline, in order to combat the destructive, deadly forces of oppression that operate under the supervision and approval of the state. Direct action is therefore as much a creative process, exploring new ways of promoting freedom and liberation, as it is a form of resistance to oppression.

In an attempt to radicalize animal theology, we must also recognize the ways in which all forms of oppression are uniquely connected to one another.

Animal exploitation does not exist in isolation, and radical animal theologians must see that it is impossible to achieve animal liberation without also dismantling other systems of oppression, including racism, sexism, heterosexism, ableism, classism, and any other ideology that extends from what feminist scholars call the "logic of domination." To radicalize animal theology is to recognize that animal exploitation is the logical outcome of a system built on profit maximization and unlimited growth and that animal oppression shares with other forms of oppression the logic of hierarchy and domination that underpins western ways of seeing and interacting with the world. This analysis, which recognizes that animal exploitation is not simply the problem in and of itself but is in fact a symptom of a much broader problem of domination, leads us to respond to these atrocities in an altogether different fashion. This response leads radical animal theologians to go about the construction of a new world in the shell of the old and leads us to build broad-based coalitions that understand that an injury to one is truly an injury to all.

Radical animal theologians see the terrors enacted under the authority of capitalist power structures and the ways in which Christianity has been co-opted and distorted for thousands of years to aid in upholding those structures. One of the tasks of radical animal theologians is to recognize these connections and to dismantle them. Christianity has been the face of colonization, racism, and Western ideologies for over a millennia. Many have died in the name of Jesus at the hands of violent agents of the Church, who used its social and political influence to uphold systemic hierarchies and bolster the name of powerful elites. In the face of this, radical animal theologians read of the life and words of Jesus and see a man who died for what he taught. He spoke of an unrelenting love for neighbors and for the earth that stands in the face of empires and oppressive religious ideologies to promote justice and freedom for all of creation. Radical animal theologians seek to understand the aspects of the Christian tradition that uphold systems of hierarchy and domination and to simultaneously oppose those same systems with their physical bodies. In other words, a radical animal theology must oppose all forms of hierarchy and domination both in theory and in practice.

Why Radicalize Animal Theology?

Since the 1970s, animal theologians have sought to draw connections between the obvious intersections of a life that is faithful to the Christian message and the need to care for non-human animals. These animal theologians have largely taken up the task of making these connections clear and accessible to large swaths of the Christian population, forming arguments that seek to show the incompatibility of animal suffering with central tenets of the Christian tradition. While animal theologians approach the field of animal ethics from different perspectives, some focusing on the importance of certain Biblical passages, some making connections with certain theological perspectives, and others drawing from deep connections with the natural world that are present throughout the Christian tradition, their response to animal suffering is largely the same.

Many of these scholars present their case for the concern of non-human animals and then lay out, in detail, the ways in which the reader can respond by changing their theology and no longer using or supporting individuals and institutions who use animals for food, clothing, entertainment, and scientific research. These responses often focus on personal as well as corporate responsibility by bringing to light the necessity of one's withdrawal from participating in actions that exploit, hurt, and kill non-human animals and suggesting that one push for legislation and public policies that may improve the lives of non-human animals. Regardless of the animal theologian's approach, it is often the case that they operate from the assumption that animal exploitation is merely a result of our culture's consumer choices rather than a symptom of a much broader, systemic problem.

This emphasis put on consumer habits by animal theologians directly parallels the response of the contemporary animal rights movement, which uses the political system and media campaigns to promote a vegan diet alongside welfare reforms. The emphasis that animal theologians put on the individual consumer stems from a Eurocentric framework that views the capitalist system as a neutral actor whose participation in the mutilation of non-human animals is a result of the demand of the consumer rather than the logical outcome of a system built on unlimited growth and profit maximization.

Insisting that non-human animals are not mere objects to be used and consumed by human beings, animal theologians largely ascribe to a rights-based approach to animal ethics. In parallel with the contemporary animal rights movement, however, their Eurocentric approach to animal liberation forces animal theologians to focus on vegan education and political reform rather than allowing them to construct an ethic that significantly challenges the broader systemic nature of the problem. Their willingness to appeal to the masses by distancing themselves from anything that would undoubtedly challenge the status quo leads them to the same failures of the contemporary animal rights movement.

In an attempt to distance his work from the "moral zeal" of the radical animal rights movement and the Animal Liberation Front (ALF) more broadly, prominent animal theologian and founder of the Oxford Centre for Animal Ethics, Andrew Linzey (1987), argues that this "tormented minority" will seek change at any cost, even if that cost includes "murder and terrorism" (pg. 100). Although Linzey is one of the most well-known and celebrated animal theologians in modern history, he seems to have a shallow understanding of the intentions and goals of the ALF. The Eurocentrism from which Linzey gleans his ethical and theological foundation forces him to use the same language as the state in describing them as self-righteous terrorists whose moral concern does not extend beyond the non-human animal world. While Linzey is careful to use quotes that serve to bolster his claims, he fails to mention that the ALF has never harmed anyone, and takes "all necessary precautions against harming any animal, human and non-human," as an essential ALF guideline (cited in Best & Nocella, 2004, pg. 8).

Although Linzey has written about the connections between human and non-human oppression, within his critique of radical animal rights groups lies what seems to be an assumption that animal liberation is something that is altogether separate from other struggles for liberation. This leads him to make dismissive claims about the nature of violence without ever having to listen to or engage in conversations about community self-defense, acting in defiance to unjust laws, or creating safe spaces for oppressed communities by directly challenging systems of power through direct action, disruption, and economic sabotage. While animal theologians rightly suggest that we cannot change the world for non-human animals without challenging the ways that we have come to view them as expendable and disposable, the same is true for our assumptions about the nature of private property, academic elitism, non-violence, social change, and hierarchy and domination in general. Animal theologians must therefore begin their approach to animal liberation by first recognizing that animal suffering is a result of the very same logic of domination that is at the root of all oppression.

For animal theologians to invest so much of their time developing theological frameworks that promote the welfare of non-human animals, it is illogical to distance themselves from decentralized groups like the ALF, who not only seek to dismantle speciesism but also the very logic of hierarchy and domination from which our speciesist tendencies arise. For animal theologians such as Linzey to distance themselves from actions that directly liberate animals and help to shine light on the ways in which violence and domination are embedded within the capitalist system, is to drastically overlook the necessity of such actions in any attempt to bring about liberation for both human and non-humans.

This attempt to delegitimize the radical approach to total liberation, as practiced by radical Earth and animal rights activists, acts as a barrier that helps to separate Linzey's work from any ideology that stands in stark contrast to the status quo. Linzey's work and his half-hearted critique of the ALF serves as an example of the failure of animal theology to break free from the constraints of the dominant narrative and instead does whatever possible to maintain legitimacy within that very system. Rather than address the broader problems of hierarchy and domination that lead to animal exploitation, animal theologians quickly fall victim to and mirror the single-issue campaigns of the contemporary animal rights movement by focusing on non-human animal suffering at the expense of broader struggles with which they share affinity.

Animal theologians have held onto the idea that the capitalist system and the logic of domination that it represents is not broken but is misguided. In true liberal fashion, they see themselves as arbiters of change, voices of reason, and catalysts that will ignite a new era of ethical concern for non-human animals. This conviction leads one to believe that the system is neutral in the face of injustice, and that with enough support and public pressure, the system will bend to the needs and desires of the people. Yet, scholars of color, feminist scholars, queer scholars, and many more have always pointed out the inconsistencies of this conviction and have time and time again showed that a system built on unlimited growth and profit maximization is far from neutral in regards to their struggles for liberation. Rather than seeking to dismantle capitalism, animal theologians have consistently legitimized the very same systems of power that many marginalized communities have claimed central to their oppression.

It is in this light that we suggest that animal theology will consistently fail in its quest for liberation if it does not take seriously the roots of the problem, which are informed by a logic of hierarchy and domination. If animal theology is to construct an ethic that is truly liberative for non-human animals, it must extend from a deep concern for the voices of those on the margins, engage in praxis that delegitimizes systems of power, open up new networks of communication with those involved in other struggles for liberation, and help to build power from below. We feel that the best way for animal theologians to begin exploring what a radical animal theology might look like is to reflect on Christian movements of the past that have implemented similar approaches to their struggles for liberation and to put them in conversation with radical Earth and animal rights groups that have a similar approach to animal liberation.

What a Radical Animal Theology Might Look Like

Though confirming sources are hard to come across, we have heard tales of Quaker communities providing prison support for some of the first ALF actions in history. Though these allegations may seem suspicious given Linzey's previous portrayal of the ALF, a Quaker community rising in support of direct action taken to directly combat animal oppression should come as no surprise. Quaker communities are known for their commitment to non-violence and overall interest in social justice, and connecting issues of human violence with the violence inflicted upon non-human animals is no large leap.

As the stories go, this Christian community witnessed the actions of these activists and understood that their actions, although illegal in the eyes of the state, were done in order to liberate animals from oppression, torture, and death. As a community committed to non-violence, the Quakers supported the activists because they understood that their motivations laid in a concern for the welfare of animals and for the natural world. Finding affinity with these activists, the Quaker community recognized that the direct action that these activists had taken on behalf of the animals challenged the very same systems of violence and domination that they were seeking to dismantle.

This story, no matter how factual it may be, unintentionally introduces an analysis of power that we believe must be taken seriously by radical animal theologians. This analysis reveals a very different approach to the way that we talk about violence when constructing a liberative ethic than what Linzey offers in his critique. While Linzey is clear that actions intended to physically stop, dismantle, or destroy private property are, in his view, violent, the Quakers in the story view the lives affected by this "private property" as more important than the property itself. The animal activists and their supporters, such as this community of Quakers, saw the lives of non-human animals to be much more valuable than the property that was destroyed in order to liberate them. One position views animal oppression as the result of consumer choices and the logical outcome of a morally bankrupt society, while the other recognizes animal oppression as the result of a logic of domination that is embedded in and reinforced by other forms of oppression in our society. This subtle shift in the way that these two positions analyze power and oppression directly affects what actions they consider to be nonviolent and ultimately affects the way that they view ALF direct action.

Our attempt to introduce a radical animal theology takes seriously this distinction in one's approach to animal suffering and suggests that like the story, we should support the direct tactics used by groups like the ALF. With this analysis of power, radical animal theologians recognize that the only means to liberation for human and non-human animals is to push back against all manifestations of violence in our society, and that those invested in the dominant, Eurocentric narrative will inevitably characterize any real opposition to its very existence as "violent." Rather than using this story as a platform to show that radical animal theologians must stand in solidarity with and show support for the actions of groups like the ALF, we want to suggest that radical animal theologians must move beyond mere support for groups that engage in direct action for animals. They themselves must also be willing to put their bodies on the line.

Throughout Christian history, one can find examples of Christians moving beyond symbolic acts of disobedience that appeal to the powers that be towards a more radical form of direct action. In 17th century Britain, Gerrard Winstanley and his followers occupied public lands in an attempt to repurpose the land for crop cultivation and the redistribution of resources amongst the community. These "True Levelers," or "Diggers," as they would later become known, advocated for the rights of the poor and common people in the midst of great social and political unrest in the country (Bradstock, 1997). The Diggers did not appeal to the King nor any earthly authority, but out of concern for their neighbors, they acted in a way that would directly meet their needs while simultaneously delegitimizing hierarchical power.

Winstanley's conviction that no one had the right to hoard land at the expense of their neighbors led him and his followers not to commit acts of symbolism meant to appeal to those in authority but to undermine that very authority by meeting the needs of the community directly. The legacy of the Diggers lives on in the archives of leftist political history, but it should also be remembered as a rich piece of Christian history as well. Winstanley (1649) wrote of the Earth being created by God as a "Common Treasury" that has been hoarded and possessed in the hands of a few (para. 5). Biblically, God's original intention was for humankind to live freely and peaceably with the rest of God's creation, yet, as Winstanley writes, the rich and powerful divide the land amongst themselves, leaving the land ravaged and the poor hungry. Thus the Diggers created a theology that was grounded in praxis; the needs of the community and of the Earth was a divine charge that they upheld in the face of potential state repercussions. Radical animal theologians have a legacy to look back upon, a legacy of direct action and defiance of oppression in order to create justice and liberation for human and non-human animals alike.

Continuing this legacy of radical faith-based resistance to oppression, two Catholic Worker activists took part in actions on Election Day in 2016 and later in March of 2017 that will be most relevant to our appeal for a radical animal theology. In July of 2017, two women associated with the Des Moines, Iowa, Catholic Worker publicly confessed to arson and sabotage in their efforts to slow down the construction of the Dakota Access pipeline. Jessica Reznicek and Ruby Montoya, motivated by the actions of the anti-nuclear Plowshares movement and the beliefs of the Catholic Worker movement, determined that the only way to actively resist the destructive force of the oil pipeline was to break federal laws by destroying equipment in order to dismantle infrastructure that "poses a threat to human life and liberty" (Montoya & Reznicek, 2017c). Their actions were inspired by many of the radical Earth and environmental activists who have implemented economic sabotage and property destruction as a tool for liberation. In a public statement, Reznicek (July 25, 2017) tells us that the two came forward publicly with their action "to empower others to act boldly, with purity of heart, to dismantle the infrastructures which deny us our rights to water, land and liberty." She goes on to state, "We, as civilians, have seen the repeated failures of the government, and it is our duty to act with responsibility and integrity, risking our own liberty for the sovereignty of us all" (Montoya & Reznicek, 2017b).

Reznicek and Montoya exhausted every legal avenue available to them that would serve as an appeal to those in positions of power. They quickly discovered, however, that attending public hearings, requesting Environmental Impact Statements, participating in acts of civil disobedience, attending marches and rallies, participating in hunger strikes, and participating in boycotts and encampments fell on deaf ears (Montoya & Reznicek, 2017a). As activists like Reznicek and Montoya participated in these legal actions that were meant to appeal to the power of the state, those same powers were simultaneously giving corporations permission to brutalize the land, water, and people in an attempt to minimize dissent and maintain their public image. The two activists, beginning to see that the system is broken and does not listen to the demands of the people, recognized the necessity for radical direct action. Teaching themselves how to destroy pipeline valves, after a great deal of discernment, Reznicek and Montoya took action. Their acts of sabotage and later acts of arson halted construction for weeks, providing themselves and others in the community with time to recuperate, regroup, and re-strategize in their attempts to halt the construction of such a disastrous pipeline.

In the end, the construction of the Dakota Access pipeline was completed amidst massive public outrage, including the largest Native American protest of this century at Standing Rock reservation. But the actions of these two activists, and the countless others who committed acts of direct action during the construction of the pipeline, have helped to shine light on the true nature of the capitalist system. While liberal and progressive theologians have consistently bought into the illusion that it is possible to reform systems of power meant to protect the private interests of a few and maintain control of the masses, like many radical Christians before them, Reznicek and Montoya act as prophetic witnesses showing the world that the brave actions of a few who are willing to take matters into their own hands are far more effective than age-old tactics meant to sway the opinions of the political and economic elite.

The theme of direct action and radical attempts at dismantling oppression from a Christian perspective can be found in the above examples and in many actions carried out by Christian communities such as the anti-war Catonsville Nine and the Milwaukee Fourteen of the 1960s, the Plowshares movement, and many other unnamed direct actions and campaigns. Radical animal theologians can and must learn from the works of Christian activists who have acted upon their convictions in order to fulfill God's call for peace and liberation and glean tactical insights from marginalized communities whose experience of oppression leads them to take action against systems of hierarchy and domination.

Similarly, we can learn from animal activist groups who historically and presently engage in direct action for the sake of animal liberation. This includes individuals and organizations such as the ALF, Sea Shepherd Conservation Society, Hunt Saboteurs Association (HSA), and Project FANG. These are organizations dedicated to the liberation of animals, whether it be whaling or poaching, fox hunting, animal testing, or animal agriculture. Some organizations like the ALF, Sea Shepherd, and HSA actively engage in sabotage, property destruction, and animal liberation. Some of the actions are done by disturbing the day-to-day activities of animal industry. Sea Shepherd ships use tactics to disable vessels and prevent them from hunting marine wildlife. HSA activists interrupt hunting by confusing hunting dogs with smells and sounds and by locking gates or other disruptive actions. The ALF is a broad-based, autonomous organization that uses a multitude of tactics which vary from cell to cell to liberate animals by directly releasing them from facilities, destroying laboratories and factories, providing veterinary care, and rehoming non-human animals in need. Other organizations like Project FANG offer support for imprisoned animal liberationists by offering traveling expenses for friends and family, advocating for prisoners' rights, and providing emotional and financial support to the prisoners. One can witness the incredible impact that these organizations and the individuals who participate in direct action have on the lives of non-human animals across the world. Though there are certainly areas that could be improved upon, the work of these groups is truly liberative.

Our hope is that animal theologians will learn from the rich history of radical Christian resistance to oppression and state power and acknowledge the works of radical animal rights activists and the effectiveness of their direct action tactics. Radical animal theology encourages animal theologians to not only learn from those who have paved the way for more radical acts of liberation, but it also emphasizes the potential for animal theologians to contribute to these actions and add to the conversation of radical animal studies. Imagine the direct effect that radical animal theology could have in the global efforts of those engaged in resistance to state power, oppression, and violence if it supported and participated in direct action for the human and non-human alike.

Conclusion

While our proposal and push for a radical animal theology is far from complete, our brief appeal to shift animal theology away from an embrace of the status quo to a radical critique of the logic of domination that underpins Western, Eurocentric modes of thinking is intended to open up new possibilities for the field of animal theology. To use the language of one of the most prolific Christian ethicists of our time, Dr. Miguel De La Torre (2010), animal theologians have often found themselves attempting to pour new wine into the "old wineskins of Eurocentric ethics" (pg. x). Their insistence upon utilizing dominant ethical frameworks to construct a liberative ethic for non-human animals has led to the legitimization of broader systemic problems. Our push for a radical animal theology is one that takes seriously the actions of radical Christian communities of the past, tapping into those movements within the history of Christianity that recognize the need for deep, revolutionary change. Simultaneously, we have brought to light current attempts by radical Earth and animal rights groups who apply a similar approach to their struggles for animal liberation. Radical animal theology emerges at the place of convergence between the trajectory of Christian history and current struggles for liberation that attempt to strike at the root of our societal problems. Our hope is that others use this as a starting place to explore new possibilities in constructing an animal theology that is truly liberative for humans and non-humans alike.

We feel strongly that real change is possible, but those who aspire to such things must create space for a world in which real revolutionary change can begin to manifest. In this light, we feel it would be impractical and hypocritical if we were to end this project without providing concrete actions that radical animal theologians can take to help create space for such change. While this list is by no means exhaustive or complete, we believe that there are four concrete strategies that radical animal theologians can take to participate in the liberation of non-human animals.

1. *Reject capitalism and the dominant theological justifications for it*: Capitalism is an economic system based on unlimited growth and the maximization of profit and is the direct result of the logic of domination that underpins Eurocentric modes of thinking. This system of exploitation, which encompasses everything from the exploitation of workers to the over extraction of natural resources and abuse of non-human animals, has largely been supported by theologically motivated justifications for the acquisition and abuse of power. Any attempt to sway the opinions of the broader Christian community toward non-human animals must resist the temptation to make the claim that animal liberation is compatible with dominant theological justifications for power and domination.

2. *Reject veganism as an end in itself*: While we recognize the importance of refraining from participating in systems that exploit non-human animals, we also recognize that abstinence from such practices is not liberative in and of itself. Any appeal to veganism that is not backed by a broader understanding of resistance to oppression quickly loses traction when it is not tied to broader revolutionary struggles. The end result of such a project is the illusion of a just capitalist system that takes seriously the ethical demands of the consumer. Such an outcome merely shifts exploitation around, finding new ways to exploit workers, non-human animals and the Earth while presenting itself as blameless.

3. *Build broad-based coalitions*: The end goal for the radical animal theologian is collective liberation. Our commitment to and involvement in other struggles for liberation directly impacts how effective we are in our pursuit for animal liberation. In recognizing the deep connections between all forms of oppression, radical animal theologians must put in the work of building broad support for collective struggles against hierarchy and domination. This includes opening themselves up to vulnerable critique and insights from communities engaged in other forms of anti-oppression work.

4. *Support and utilize direct action tactics*: Christians are no strangers to "acting as if one is already free," to cite Graeber again. After all, we are the first to proclaim that freedom comes from the spirit of Christ, not Caesar. The radical animal theologian recognizes that direct

action builds power from below while simultaneously delegitimizing the logic of domination imbedded within the dominant culture. As a result, the radical animal theologian supports and utilizes direct action tactics as an important and necessary tool to build counter power and bring about God's peaceable kingdom on Earth.

References

Best, S., & Nocella, A. J. (2004). *Terrorists or freedom fighters? Reflections on the liberation of animals.* New York, NY: Lantern Books.

Bradstock, A. (1997). *Faith in the revolution: The political theologies of Muntzer and Winstanley.* London, UK: SPCK Press.

De La Torre, M. (2010). *Latina/o social ethics: Moving beyond Eurocentric moral thinking.* Waco, TX: Baylor University Press.

Graeber, D. (2009). *Direct action: An ethnography.* Oakland, CA: AK Press.

Linzey, A. (1987). *Christianity and the rights of animals.* London, UK: SPCK Publishing.

Montoya, R., & Reznicek, J. (2017a). After having explored and exhausted all avenues of process . . . [Public Statement]. Retrieved from http://www.mississippistand.com/

Montoya, R., & Reznicek, J. (2017b). 'We acted from our hearts': Activists in Iowa admit to repeatedly sabotaging Dakota Access pipeline [Public Statement]. Retrieved from https://www.democracynow.org/2017/7/25/activists_in_iowa_admit_to_repeatedly

Montoya, R., & Reznicek, J. (2017c). Meet the two Catholic workers who secretly sabotaged the Dakota Access pipeline to halt construction. Interview by Amy Goodman [Video Recording]. Democracy Now! Retrieved from https://www.democracynow.org/2017/7/28/meet_the_two_catholic_workers_who

Soelle, D. (1999). *Against the wind: Memoir of a radical Christian.* Minneapolis, MN: Augsburg Fortress.

Winstanley, G. (1649). The true lLvellers standard advanced: Or, the state of the community opened, and present to the sons of man. Retrieved from https://www.marxists.org/reference/archive/winstanley/1649/levellers-standard.htm

5. Days of War, Knights of Tempeh: Anarchism, Animal Liberation & Social War

MICHAEL LOADENTHAL

Introduction

The interplay and symbiosis connecting anarchism and animal liberation is well established, and discussions on their interaction have become a mainstay of anarchist convergences. Talks on "anarchism and animal liberation" are regularly hosted at bookfairs and exemplified in a recent talk given by Josh Harper and Scott Crow (*The Talon Conspiracy*, 2013). In this talk, the speakers—both established anarcho-activists in their own right—detailed their personal journeys amongst the intersecting communities of those opposing the state and those fighting against speciesism. Such narratives of subcultural overlap and shared politics are common throughout the contemporary era of a reinvigorated struggle of direct attack by clandestine, decentralized networks of saboteurs, arsonists, and vandals. The following chapter aims to paint a picture of modern anarchist combat as it interacts with efforts to smash the machinery of animal abuse and the capital it generates. The historical examples will be taken from the period between 1999 and 2014—the post-'*Battle in Seattle*', post-9/11 period coinciding with the reemergence of the urban guerilla that had largely disappeared following the 1980s. In order to develop the history, this chapter will detail a series of attacks claimed by underground, anarchist-aligned networks, and whenever possible, discussed through the attacker(s)' own words.

Intersectional, Non-Reformist, Anti-Speciesists

Anarchists and animal liberationists obviously share quite a bit in common in terms of their philosophical underpinnings. In one of the earliest linkages, anarchist Peter Kropotkin spoke of the mutualism and cooperative tendencies in non-human animals. In *Mutual Aid: A Factor of Evolution* (1902), Kropotkin argues that cooperation is a primary factor in species' abilities to survive the evolutionary process. Kropotkin likens the 'naturally'-occurring mutualism of beetles, crabs, termites, ants and bees to the 'natural' tendency for humans to act together for the benefit of the collective (1902, Chapters 1–2). Anarchists and anti-speciesists share a tendency towards decentralization, mutual aid (including that provided to those in captivity), voluntary association, opposition to the state and capitalism, and the rejection of mediated forms of representative governance. While reformist, *rights*-based organizations such as People for the Ethical Treatment of Animals (PETA) may share a rejection of speciesism, the commonality ends there as the membership-based organization does not share the other hallmarks of anarchist-aligned, direct action movements such as the Animal Liberation Front (ALF).

Anarchist anti-speciesists have been at the forefront of critiquing the reformist nature of more traditional animal rights campaigners. In one example, anarchists distributed leaflets and dropped a banner coinciding with a PETA event. The communiqué announcing the action states:

> This action was prompted by a call-out for turkey leafleting made by PETA . . . [who] asked that their activists 'dress conservatively' and 'stand up straight and hold signs prominently'. Their blatant classism and conservatism wasn't surprising. (Anonymous, 2012a)

The anarchists' banner read "Total Liberation: None Are Free Until All Are Free," a sentiment reflective of the anti-reformist, intersectional nature of anti-state politics. Other anarchist-aligned collectivities have articulated *total liberationist* positions. One particularly interesting example is that of the (now defunct) anarcho-insurrectionary-Queer network Bash Back! (BB!). On 4 March 2010, in response to the killing of a Sea World trainer by an orca whale, a BB! cell issued a communiqué:

> The nonhuman political prisoners at Sea World Orlando have organized the first chapter of Splash Back!, an insurrectionary tendency of sea animals dedicated to destroying all forms of oppression. Bash Back! must be allies in the struggle for animal liberation, as well as against the religious right which has sought to criminalize the bodies of queers and orcas for so long . . . the time for sea animal liberation is now. Solidarity with all Trainer Killers. (Bash Back!, 2010)

While the communiqué is certainly penned as satire, it makes the case for an anarchist-derived, total liberationist politic. In short, the author(s) argue that to be in favor of Queer liberation is to align oneself on the side of those fighting domination—in this case, captive sea animals (Loadenthal, 2011). BB! argues that to be *pro-Queer* necessarily positions the individual as anti-speciesist, anti-abelist, etc. BB!'s endorsement of the trainer's killing can thus be seen as a nod to a more comprehensive manner of intersectionality—a total liberationist ethic which, unlike the efforts of reformists, refuses to adopt classist, racist and/or sexist positions in furtherance of an animal rights agenda.

BB!'s position is one of presumption; the network *presumes* that to be in solidarity one must oppose all forms of domination. For example, in 2013, French activists painted a mural expressing solidarity between movements for animals and those opposing far-right/neo-Nazis. The mural is in response to the murder of Clément Méric, a "vegan anti-fascist activist" by a "far-right activist" involved locally in animal rights events. The communiqué announcing the mural states:

> Our message is clear, the Animal Liberation Movement was, is and will always be antifascist. We will not tolerate racism, sexism and homophobia and that is a very big concern for every person that truly cares about this cause. We do ask to every person involved in the animal rights movement in France and everywhere in the world to fiercely stand up against racism, sexism and homophobia. The far-right politics don't match with animal liberation and that will never change. (Anonymous, 2013h)

Similar to the BB! communiqué, the French activists' position is that to stand on the side of animal liberation *must* translate into an opposition towards fascism, racism, sexism and homophobia, both within social movements and the larger society.

In a final example, one can examine the positions of the public face of clandestine animal liberationists—the North American Animal Liberation Press Office and then officer Nicoal Sheen (2013)—the central distributors of ALF and allied communiqués. In August 2013, NAALPO (2013) distributed their "Summer E-Newsletter" including a call to support recently jailed soldier-turned-whistle-blower Chelsea Manning. The solidarity request featured a photograph of *Chelsea*—a male-to-female transgender person—and refers to the prisoner using female pronouns. Though far from an anarcho-animal liberationist, Manning's inclusion as a NAALPO-advertised political prisoner demonstrates a politic of solidarity and support for not only whistleblowers facing repression, but also transgender individuals struggling against transphobic prisons. Manning's inclusion in the newsletter is a sign of the presumed intersectionality of the ALF and its supporter constituency.

Animal Liberation & Anarchist Direct Action

Most commonly, the anarchist-liberationist connection comes in the form of movement overlap. It has been common for anarchist projects to work towards liberationist goals—such as Food Not Bombs—and it has been equally common for explicitly animal-centric campaigns to borrow tactics, strategies, messaging, and participants from the wider anarchist social movement. In their various formulations, ALF activists have described themselves as anarchists, while anarchists have spoken out against speciesism. On 16 July 2013, an ALF cell vandalized a fur store and then proceeded to give equal treatment to the homes of two employees. In their communiqué, the author(s) self-label as "anarchists in San Diego," yet sign the document as the "Animal Liberation Front" (ALF, 2013). Similarly, after vandalizing a butcher shop, activists in Chile signed their communiqué "health and anarchy!" (Anonymous, 2013f). Incidents such as this are quite common, and if one browses communiqué repositories of the ALF, they are sure to find consistent reference to the broader fight against state and capital.

Political crossovers frequent in underground acts of property destruction have witnessed similar articulations in publicly-recruiting street protests. In 2002, anarchists prepared to confront the New York meetings of the World Economic Forum (WEF). These anti-globalization demonstrations shared the spotlight with the liberationist agenda. During the anti-WEF demonstrations, an aggressive march was hosted to "tour" sites affiliated with Huntington Life Sciences (HLS), a contract-based animal testing/breeding company targeted by the ALF for decades. Prior to the march, participants were urged to wear black clothing and cover their faces with masks (Anonymous, 2002). Such tactical provisions were common amongst the anarchist-led counter-summit events of the time and served to visibly separate militant, property destruction-prone anarchists from more conventional, law-abiding marchers.

During the guided tour of "HLS targets," paint projectiles were thrown and several windows smashed by marchers targeting an Upper East Side apartment where corporate staff resided (Schurr, 2002). One of the marchers, Benjamin Persky, was arrested and served two years in connection to the broken windows of Parker Quillan, CEO of Quilcap Hedge fund, a top HLS shareholder. Following repeated targeting by activists, Quilcap eventually cut their ties with HLS. During the anti-WEF march, not only was an anarchist counter-summit used as the venue for an anti-animal testing campaign's protest, but the wider anarchist community helped to facilitate a hero's welcome for Persky following his sentence (Animal Defense League, 2004;

Anonymous, 2004). These sorts of hybridized movements have become hallmarks of both scenes. In Washington DC, the most visible anarchist collective and the most visible animal liberation group have often allied to host demonstrations. On Halloween 2012, Anarchist Alliance DC and Defending Animal Rights Today & Tomorrow (DARTT) hosted a night march, "anticapitalist trick or treating … visiting the homes of key executives involved in everything from taking homes away from people to the heartless monsters who do business with [HLS]" (DARTT, 2012).

Beyond the US, a historical recounting of Israeli anarchism authored by CrimethInc. (2013) noted that within the evolution of domestic anarchist networks, the animal rights/liberation movement helped to infuse participants and maintain social networks. The social ties built around anarchist campaigning—including that opposing Israeli occupation of Palestine—fed an animal rights movement that at times served to "recruit people for clandestine [ALF] activities" (pfm, 2013). Furthermore, according to movement historians, such symbiotic functioning did not end there: "Just as the animal rights movement was kick-started by anarchists, Anarchists Against the Wall was in turn conceived by animal rights activists" (pfm, 2013). Within this account, if one were to order these movements linearly, anarchists build the animal rights movement that in turn brings anarchists further into the fight against military occupation. Such organically-occurring, mutually-beneficial, cooperative symbioses occur frequently. Just as a great number of anarchists are vegans, so too are a large number of vegans self-labeled anarchists.

Insurrectionary Anti-Speciesism

From amongst the larger anarchist movement, a tendency is present which rejects broad-based movement building efforts seen as a hallmark of the traditional Left. What has come to be known as insurrectionary anarchism, nihilist anarchism, and the making of Social War, is held up as a stern tide of resistance in light of more mediated, reformist, and civil (i.e. law-abiding) anarchisms (Anonymous, 2013a). Interestingly, with the rise of insurrectionary networks of attack—as best embodied in the Informal Anarchist Federation (FAI), International Revolutionary Front (IRF), and Conspiracy of Cells of Fire (CCF)—these tendencies have grown, become increasingly active, and deteritorialized their efforts.

In 2013, hundreds of vandalisms, sabotages, arsons, bombings and other forms of resistance were cooked up by an underground, decentralized network of individuals, striking in anonymity, and self-reporting through the opacity of the Internet. Alongside the rise of insurrectionary attacks, there has been a frequent mixing of animal liberation and abolitionist mindsets. This trend—one wherein anarchists are confronting speciesism in their actions and animal liberationists are taking strikes against the state—is persistent within the amorphous insurrectionary movement that has seen a rise in the post-millennial era. Through English-language websites such as "325. nostate," "War on Society" and "Act for Freedom Now!", communiqués are translated and circulated rapidly. The remainder of this chapter explores the overlap between emergent networks of insurrectionary attack and those of direct action animal liberation. Here we will examine how the FAI/IRF/CCF meets the ALF, and through an incident-based chronology, we can explore patterns of not only action, but tactical learning, strategy, rhetoric and targeting.

The movements of the ALF/FAI have frequently shown cross-pollinated *tactical* learning. For example, the tactic of product contamination, utilized in ALF circles since the 1980s, has recently seen use by insurrectionists. In November 2013, liberationists reported to have damaged Kiwi-brand leather polish containing mink oil. The activists' claimed to target Kiwi for their "involvement in the fur trade" (Anonymous, 2013j) and reportedly added cyanic acid to 263 units before placing them back on shelves. In response, S.C. Johnson was forced to recall large portions of stock to "protect" consumers' shoes from damage that would have resulted from the adulterated polish. As a result of the costly recall, S.C. Johnson announced that they would remove mink oil as a component in the polish. Furthermore, Kiwi is no small target controlling 74% of the market, with 2012 sales of $129 million (Ng & Binkley, 2013). Less than a month after the action against Kiwi, a Grecian FAI cell carried out a product contamination targeting Coca-Cola as part of their "Green Nemesis" campaign. In the FAI's communiqué, the author(s) speak to these crossovers, stating: "FAI opens up a new perspective, inviting the comrades of the anti-civilization tension and the direct action cells of ELF and ALF to perform a general international revenge and attack against the ones, who murder our lives" (FAI/IRF Nicola and Alfredo Cell, 2013). Such a tactical tributary may indicate an increasing willingness for anti-statists to adopt the methods that have often been successful for the ALF.

Amongst the insurrectionary-ALF alliance, beyond simply a tactically-shared toolset is a shared strategic vision. The liberationist campaign against HLS, embodied in the Stop Huntingdon Animal Cruelty (SHAC) campaign, has popularized the targeting of secondary and tertiary targets in an effort to isolate the animal supplier:

> The idea was to focus specifically on the corporation's finances, utilizing the tactics that had closed small businesses to shut down an entire corporation.

Activists set out to isolate HLS by harassing anyone involved with any corporation that did business with them ... The SHAC campaign set about depriving HLS of its support structure ... Secondary and tertiary targeting works because the targets do not have a vested interest in continuing their involvement with the primary target. There are other places they can take their business, and they have no reason not to do so. (Marut, 2009)

Such a strategy of identifying key economic and logistical choke points can be linked to numerous anarchist thinkers including the infamous anti-technology, quasi-anarchist militant Ted Kaczynski, popularly known as the "Unabomber." In an essay entitled "Hit Where It Hurts," the jailed Kaczynski called for a similar strategy arguing that the uncoordinated vandalism of targets such as fast food chains—which commonly occurs within ALF campaigns—constitutes a non-revolutionary and "pointless" act (2010, p. 249). Instead of striking these more prominent targets, Kaczynski encourages strategic planning, targeting the system at large, and urges clandestine saboteurs: "Work effectively toward the elimination of the technoindustrial system, revolutionaries must attack the system at points at which it cannot afford to give ground. They must attack the vital organs of the system" (Kaczynski, 2010, p. 253). Kaczynski should be considered by anarchists with a great degree of caution as some of his work invokes racist, misogynist, and authoritarian tendencies alongside condemnations of the "Left." Despite his many shortcomings, Kaczynski is a recurrent touchpoint in some contemporary militant milieus challenging systems of ecocide and domestication.

While Kaczynski is certainly not a central point of influence for the contemporary anarchist milieu, his effect cannot be discounted as his name has become an increasingly common reference by those attacking the systems of technological domination and speciesism, especially those active in Mexico. For example, the underground entity known as Individualists Tending Toward the Wild/Savage (ITS) has led an aggressive campaign of bombs, bullets, and fire to target nanotechnologists and others seen as perpetuating the techno-industrial society. In at least five communiqués (2011a, b, c, 2012, 2013), ITS speaks of Kaczynski's influence. Other ideologically-aligned, Mexico-based, eco-insurrectionists such as the Terrorist Cell for the Direct Attack—Anticivilization Faction (TCfDA) have carried out similar attacks which include references to the Unabomber. In a September 2011 communiqué claiming responsibility for multiple bombing, TCfDA references Kaczynski, acknowledging that they are not "revolutionaries" in the traditional sense but instead advocate:

Violent direct action as a means of attacking a small part of the problem ... it is necessary to attack those directly responsible for the artificialization of the

wild since they are the ones who hold inside their heads the information and
the potentiality for this artificialization to be realized. (Células Terroristas Por
el Ataque Directo—Facción Anticivilizadora, 2011)

Thus Kaczynski, as one point in the anarcho past, has a notable influence on
the contemporary period of struggle closely aligned with the insurrectionary
tendency. Kaczynski's influence may be only a small point, but such overlaps
are common throughout all manners of militant resistance against the state
and speciesism.

For biographical examples, one can examine the state's "sentencing
memorandum" outlining the personal political histories of members of "The
Family," the largest ALF-ELF cell to be exposed. According to state's evidence (Immergut, Engdall, Peifer, & Ray, 2007), ALF-ELF cell members
Daniel McGowan, Nathan Block, Joyanna Zacher and Suzanne Savoire participated in the 1999 Seattle black bloc early in their campaign of eco-animal
arson and sabotage. This crossover has not escaped the observant eyes of state
security forces. In numerous cases exposed by the *Guardian*, police infiltra-
tors have immersed themselves within British ALF cells through participation with more law-abiding animal rights and environmental campaigns.

In determining *whom* to target in direct action campaigns, the ALF has
attacked explicitly statist sites, further showing the ideological congruence
amongst those fighting the state and those primarily focused on ending animal exploitation. In one such example, a Canadian ALF cell attacked a police
car with a Molotov cocktail. The vehicle was chosen for its proximity to a
fur store, and according to the attackers "was parked there to intimidate
or detour [sic] any future attacks" (Anonymous, 2013c). The communiqué
states, "Make no mistake, this is war. This is a fur war. This is a class war"
(Anonymous, 2013c). For this cell, there is a presumption of agreement that
those targeting the fur industry would also be in support of attacks against
the state, and more specifically, its violent enforcers of social order—police.

In another communiqué, activists claiming responsibility for the targeting of prison vehicles conclude with the words, "this small attack was
done with all the caged animals & humans at the for-front of our minds"
(Anonymous, 2013d). In a communiqué distributed through a prominent
pro-ALF website, "Anonymous Anarchists" (2013) claimed an attack on a
seafood restaurant. In Illinois, the "Chicago Veganarchist Wolf" (2013) carried out multiple attempted arsons of a Burger King, leaving stickers behind
reading "Oppressor Be Warned (A)." In one final example, Philadelphia anarchists responded to the police's killing of dogs with graffiti, writing: "we
hold nothing but contempt for those who choose to be police and for those
who abuse animals" (Anarchists, 2013).

Beyond outright cross-community targeting, there are frequent allusions to ALF-styled direct action included in the rhetoric and propaganda of the globalized anarcho-insurrectionary struggle. In a sense, these communiqué author(s) are attempting to inspire action through imagery derived from the successful campaigns of the ALF/ELF. In one example, a British FAI cell writes:

> Animals are liberated, bio-science laboratories burnt down. Transgenic crops trashed and business people intimidated. Banks and courthouses are blown up, judges shot and stabbed. Police and their stations are attacked with Molotovs, sticks, dynamite, firearms. Energy supplies are disrupted, television infrastructure attacked, internet cables and mobile-phone masts sabotaged. (International FAI, 2011)

Such a chain of phantasmagorias has an obvious historical reference in the actions of the ALF/ELF and their campaigns of animal liberations, arsons, and destruction of GMO crops. These are mixed alongside the more aggressive tactics involving bombs, bullets and knives, which have risen in prominence with the insurrectionary turn.

Greece & Turkey [2011–2013]

In the Mediterranean locales of Greece and Turkey, while there has been a consistent campaign against the state and capital, attacks targeting the mechanisms of species domination have been less common. However, in Greece, a series of at least four actions occurring between December 2011-February 2013 placed insurrectionary politics and animal liberation together. Greece occupies a very particular position within the larger insurrectionary movement, as it has consistently been the harbinger of the direct, unmediated attack. On 26 November 2011, what was described as an "antispeciesist demonstration" (Act for Freedom Now!, 2011) occurred. While this aboveground, public, anarchist-sponsored action is not of the type discussed in this chapter, the event was reported by a central distributor for English-language, insurrectionary communications, and during the demonstration, marchers—described in the communiqué as "combative"—threw paint bombs and scrawled graffiti on buildings including slogans such as "Arson for each fur scumbag" (Act for Freedom Now!, 2011). The demonstration was decidedly anarchist though not quite within the insurrectionary chronology.

While a daytime street demonstration is not typical of the insurrectionary tendency, the 15 August 2012 window smashing and graffiti targeting a meat market comes a bit closer. While the communiqué, signed by "Anti-speciesists" (2012), is reflective of a generalized animal liberation and anarchist politic, its translation and distribution via the "informal network of counter-information and translation" is a significant illustration of overlap between traditionalist anarchist forums and those of the insurrectionary tendency.

This tendency can also be seen in a December 2012 anti-speciesist demonstration. Just like the November march and the August attack, those that attended in December were described as "anarchists and antispeciesists" (Anonymous, 2012b). Similar to the previous protest, the demonstration is portrayed as involving paint bombs and graffiti. The report does not include the insurrectionary language adopted in communiqués, yet asserts the interconnected nature of anarchism's anti-state/capitalism and animal liberation's rejection of speciesism:

> The State/Capital shows no mercy, neither on people, nor on non-human animals, and once again its mercenaries protected the interests of exploiters. They are skinning all of us, every living being, to warm the pockets of our killers. We are at war on all fronts. (Anonymous, 2012b)

Despite Greece's historical and contemporary linkages to the most visible elements of the insurrectionary tendency, in only one communiqué that has been so far located is an interconnected, insurrectionary, animal liberationist message offered.

On 18 February 2013, a grouping calling itself a "collaboration of teams" and labeled "A.L.F.//Chaotics" (2013) attacked "various targets" near Athens. In a manner typical of the insurrectionary method of unbounded social war, the attackers struck a number of loosely-connected targets related to issues of government, institutionalized education, religion and animal abuse. During the reported incidents, the attackers spray painted, glued locks and broke windows of targets including fur/leather retailers, animal testing, "pet" stores, butcher shops, government and education services, a hunter's personal car, and the homes of specifically-targeted, animal abusing and law enforcement individuals. The communiqué's author(s) (A.L.F. // Chaotics, 2013) were sure to include shout outs to "the urban guerilla captives of C.C.F., F.A.I.-I.R.F., A.L.F., E.L.F.," highlighting their comingled and overlapping networks.

Similar to Greece, in Turkey, the other Mediterranean venue surveyed, one incident demonstrated a more traditionalist anarchist approach. In October 2013, activists in Istanbul carried out a series of nighttime graffiti focused on a host of issues including "the murder of Pavlos Fyssas in Greece, antifascism, anarchy, rebellion, animal massacre in Romania, animal liberation, and the Gezi uprising" (Anonymous, 2013i).

Bolivia [2011–2012]

Bolivia has seen an increase in activity by clandestine animal liberationists this decade. While no ALF-linked attacks were reported to communiqué distributors prior to 2011, there were at least four attacks 2011–2012 posted on *Bite Back Magazine*—a central repository for ALF attack announcements—as well as two attacks reported on *War On Society*—a central spoke in the internationalist translation and communiqué-reporting network. The animal liberation-themed attacks reported included the use of explosives (FLA Bolivia, 2011), smoke bombs (Incendiary Nucleus of Action for the spread of the revolt/FAI-FRI, 2011), sabotage (Autonomous fraction of rebel thieves FAI-FRI, 2012) and the gluing of locks (Some Wayward Nocturnals–FAI/IRF, 2012b). This included one communiqué issued in early November 2011 that announced the emergence of an ALF cell in the country. During this two-year span, there were at least ten additional communiqués issued to insurrectionary news outlets claiming attacks in Bolivia outside of an animal liberationist politic. Many of these attacks speak of solidarity with CCF/FAI/IRF and other globally-distributed networks (see for example Wrists of Fire Insurrectional Command, FAI–IRF, 2011).

Spanning the insurrectionary and liberationist frameworks, the first such incident occurs around the announcement of the ALF's first attack in country. A few days later, on 4 November 2011, the "Incendiary Nucleus of Action for the spread of the revolt/FAI-FRI" (2011) claimed responsibility for placing two smoke bombs in La Paz Burger Kings, and used their communiqué to express solidarity for insurrectionary prisoners in Mexico, Chile, Argentina, Greece and Switzerland. The authors also show support for CCF as well as the lesser-known Grecian Revolutionary Organization. The communiqué claiming the smoke bombs is filled with language showing the influence of insurrectionary anarchism, and specifically, its deep green tendencies:

> We made it clear to those who seek to domesticate us, to make us autonomatons and separate us from the wild freedom that nature provides us, that we will not give up our appetite for disruption until there is an end to every relationship based on domination, that we will empty and destroy all the cages, physical and mental, that ravage our bodies and our lives, robbing us of the potential to disobey and destroy civilization, a potential that day by day, through our actions, we are reappropriating. (Incendiary Nucleus of Action for the spread of the revolt/FAI-FRI, 2011)

Following the November incidents, the reporting of such incidents goes quiet for four months until April 2012 when "Autonomous Fraction of rebel thieves, FAI-FRI" (2012) reportedly "sabotaged" a high-end supermarket in

Cochabamba. In the communiqué, the attackers make explicit connections between human- animal struggles and state that they were motivated to act by the exploitation of workers:

> As Anti-authoritarians we will not defend a job that is dedicated to animal exploitation, that bases itself on the slavery of thousands of lives, that has as its base cages, lifelong captivity, experimentation ... Capitalism values everything in terms of the benefit that it can give. We are all part of this capitalism of consuming products that come from the exploitation of non-human animals. Animal exploitation exists because the society is speciesist and capitalism makes use of that to make an industry out of speciesism. (Autonomous Fraction of rebel thieves FAI-FRI, 2012)

The language serves to present "Workers' Day" within an animal liberationist context and argues that to fight capitalism is to fight against speciesism, as both are systems of extraction and domination.

Later that same month, in April 2012, a cell of the FAI/IRF set fire to an ATM in La Paz. While the rhetoric used to frame and relay the attack did not make any mention of an animal liberationist politic, the authors were keen to offer a sarcastic condemnation of ALF prisoner of war Walter Bond. In a postscript, the FAI/IRF writes, "all our contempt for the converted Walter Bond—pardon ... Abdul Haqq," (Some Wayward Nocturnals–FAI/IRF, 2012a), mocking the prisoner's brief conversion to Islam (before rejecting the faith and returning to an explicitly secular-anarchist position), and the adoption of an Islamicly-derived name. The following month, after speaking out against Bond, on 5 May 2012, the same FAI/IRF cell (2012b) glued locks on six businesses related to animal exploitation and the perpetuation of speciesism. Additional targets were selected because of their intersectional connections to sexual abuse, "oppressive beauty," gender hierarchies, and religion. While gluing the locks of the businesses, the vandals also affixed paper flyers to walls and windows displaying anarchist symbols and explained why the target was chosen.

Russia & Ukraine [2011–2013]

In Russia and the Ukraine, between November 2011-September 2013, activists issued nearly ten communiqués which combined some manner of the internationalist FAI/IRF with that of the ALF/ELF. In the first such communiqué, the "Earth Liberation Front (Russia)/Informal Anarchist Federation–International Revolutionary Front" (2011) express ideological affiliation and solidarity with imprisoned members of the Grecian CCF. Speaking to the nature of decentralized, moniker-linked, global networks, the Russian activists write:

As soon as we learned of existence of others like us, we started reading their [Greek CCF] texts and established rapport through claims of responsibility and mutual expressions of solidarity. It's a wonderful feeling, when one reads a text from another part of the world and yet its clear that people have same concerns, share same ideals and have same passion for freedom and social change, same rage against the status quo … [CCF was the] first group that breached the blank wall of ignorance for us. (ELF/FAI–IRF, 2011)

The writer(s) (2011) speak of a global "call for decentralized network of direct action," condemn "bourgeois-left" (i.e. civil) anarchists, and speak in praise of "the new urban guerrilla warfare … raging in our lands." If referencing the CCF and FAI/IRF as well as specific individual prisoners such as Kaczynski, Bond and Chilean anarchist bomber Luciano "Tortuga" Pitronello, the Russian ELF/FAI-IRF firmly positions themselves in line with the growing global insurrectionary attack movements throughout Europe, South America and Asia.

Nearly six months later, in May 2012, these newly-advertised networks struck in the Ukraine, by detonating a "gas bomb" in an animal crematory used to incinerate unclaimed strays (Two Sequoias, ALF-FAI, 2012). The attackers note that they were forced to change their plan when stray dogs emerged and interfered. The bombing was claimed by a new moniker, "Two sequoias, ALF, FAI/IRF," again combining the global insurrectionary tendency of the FAI/IRF with that of the ALF. The attackers note their solidarity with "imprisoned members of the CCF," as well as prisoners linked to FAI attacks in Italy, Switzerland, Indonesia and Chile. Four months later, a similar moniker emerges in Russia when "Wolfpack, ELF/ALF-Russia, FAI" (2012) claims responsibility for a series of attacks including the arson of a "meat restaurant" and cellphone tower, the liberation of 18 pheasants, and the "seed bombing" (i.e. distributing seeds through projectiles to encourage wild growth) of areas threatened with logging. The author(s) express solidarity with Russian CCF activists as well as those allied throughout Russia, Ukraine and Belarus. They also express "total support" for Mexican insurrectionary attacks networks, specifically ITS and the Insurrectional Cell—Mariano Sanchez Añon (CI-MSA) faction of the Mexican FAI (see for example CI-MSA/FAI-M, 2012).

The use of the "Wolfpack" moniker emerges in Russia again in March 2013, this time as "Wolfpack, ELF/FAI," excluding the ALF. In the March attack, carried out near Moscow, three construction vehicles were destroyed by incendiary devices (Wolfpack, ELF/FAI, 2013). The equipment was reportedly used to deliver sand to construction projects within the Khimki forest, a site of much ecological resistance. The author(s) again pay tribute to CCF/ALF/ELF/FAI as well as activists in Greece, Switzerland, Italy, Chile, the US and elsewhere. Also in March, the "Two Sequoias, ALF/FAI" (2013) reemerges to claim the liberation of a single horse, set free whilst activists were "scouting" attacks. In their brief communiqué, the author(s) do not mention the typical list of allies but do include the internationalist ALF-FAI label.

At least three more attacks occur in this spree that utilize a combined FAI-ALF name. In October 2012, "Wild Hogs, ALF-FAI" (2012) claimed the arson of an electrical substation used by hunters, and the burning of a "hunting decoy (feeding facility for boars and elks)." In July 2013, the "ALF/FAI SEALS on tour" (2013) claim the liberation of two dolphins. In this tactically-advanced incident, activists used diving equipment to enter a dolphinarium where they released animals and vandalized security equipment. In September 2013, two cells calling themselves "CCF–Russia" and "ELF–Russia" (2013) issued a joint communiqué claiming responsibility for "coordinated attacks" involving the arson of construction vehicles in Moscow. What is unique about the Russian-Ukrainian attacks is that while they routinely adopt insurrectionary monikers (e.g. CCF, FAI) combined with eco-liberationist collectivities (e.g. ELF, ALF), the attackers rarely articulate an explicitly insurrectionary politic, but instead use the communiqués to speak of more localized struggles against ecological degradation and systemic speciesism.

Interestingly, in at least two attacks, bombings were modified or canceled due to the possible injury presented to nearby dogs. This is seen in the May 2012 attack claimed by "Two Sequoias, ALF-FAI," as well as an October 2012 bombing in Russia in which the "Autonomous cell 'Silver bullets for police warewolves' of CCF RUSSIA" (2012) changed the placement of a bomb to avoid injuring a guard dog. In this attack, the author(s) explicitly adress "anarchists taken hostage by the states throughout the world" and state that "everyone who had made the choice of insurrectionary action became our brother (or sister)" (Autonomous cell "Silver bullets for police werewolves" of CCF RUSSIA, 2012).

Bristol, England [2013]

In southern England's Bristol area, three attacks in 2013 linked anarchists' rejection of law enforcement with animal liberationist politics. A few days into 2013, anonymous activists used an unsigned communiqué released to Indymedia to claim responsibility for smashing windows and spray painting parts of the Bristol Zoo. The communiqué's author(s) link the anarchist objection to prisons with a liberationist rejection of zoos:

On New Years Eve there is a tradition around the world of taking action against the prison system and showing solidarity with prisoners. We continue and extend this tradition in the spirit of total liberation for human and non-human animals alike ... They can never be everywhere and we will never accept captivity or imprisonment of any sort. (Anonymous, 2013b)

Ten days later, activists slashed tire and graffitied property belonging to prison officials. While the communiqué speaks from a prison abolitionist framework, and states that the attack targeted the property of "screws," it closes with rhetoric that links the caging of humans to that of animals. The unsigned communiqué (Anonymous, 2013d) states: "this small attack was done with all the caged animals & humans at the for-front of our minds."

Eight months later, the Bristol area was the site of a third attack. On 26 August 2013 "Angry Foxes Cell in collaboration with ACAB" (2013) set fire to the Police Firearms Training Center in Portishead. The extensive fire burned for over 12 hours. In conjunction, a separate cell slashed the tires and destroyed the paint of two vehicles owned by companies involved in prison and court services. While the targeting and language of the communiqué fits squarely within the insurrectionary tendency, the authors show linkages to a liberationist politic in two main ways. First, the chosen dual monikers of the "Angry Fox Cell" and "ACAB" (All Cops Are Bastards—a slogan of sorts for insurrectionaries) show a blending of ecological re-wilding themes and anti-police politics central to insurrectionary thought. Secondly, at the conclusion of the communiqué, the authors write:

The night of our action coincides with the announced start of the planned cull of wild badgers in the South West of England. Through attempting to facilitate the cull and stop resistance the police shore up the interests of agricultural industry and the land owning classes. We hope this will be one of many rebellions against this slaughter. Because the state and corporate security forces are integral to this world of exploitation and authority. (Angry Foxes Cell & ACAB, 2013)

This text clearly shows the influence and overlap of campaigns against systematic animal slaughter in the region, and in their final valediction, the author(s) write: "The struggle will continue until all are wild and free," speaking to a human-animal dual struggle for freedom.

Chile [2013]

During 2013, activists in Chile carried out at least four attacks blurring the lines between the insurrectionary movement of direct attack and the movement against speciesism. On 2 January 2013, the "Mauricio Morales

Incendiary Brigade" (2013) detonated an explosive device targeting a meat producer and agribusiness in Santiago. The attacker(s) write that they chose the target due to its ecological impact, and the owner's reported links to former dictator Augusto Pinochet. The attacker(s) end their communiqué with a call for "freedom" to Chilean anarchists currently on trial for bomb attacks against the state in what is known as the "Caso Security" [Security Case]. During the same month, the "Heterogeneous Faction of Libertarian Weichafes" (2013) detonated an explosive device at the headquarters of a dairy company. In their communiqué, the author(s) speak of settler colonialism, Pinochet, and the struggle of the indigenous Mapuche people. Like the January attackers, the communiqué expressed solidarity with the prisoners of the Security Case.

Approximately one months later, in late February 2013, the "Incendiary Nomad Cell" (C.N.I.) (2013) claimed responsibility for two arson attacks targeting a store accused of animal neglect and a prison headquarters. C.N.I. (2013) links the two targets, calling the prison office "these scum, stranglers of freedom, servants of the fucking authority that makes slaves of us and the animals." Nearly eight months later, Chile witnessed another arson of an animal liberationist target, this time with a communiqué linking a broader anarchist politic. The author(s) claim affiliation with ALF/ELF, condemn speciesist science and taxidermy, and call out government institutions that they call:

> The state organization responsible for animal handling, transport of laboratory animals, weak oversight of slaughterhouses, zoos and animal fairs, for perpetuating its 'normal' functioning of sales of blood per liter, and for having their own breeding vivarium. (ALF/ELF, 2013)

The author(s) conclude, calling for "animal, human and earth liberation" and write a postscript, stating, "thanks for putting your disgusting exhibition in a building owned by the state" (para. 8), once again highlighting the anarchist, anti-state influence. In other words, while the attackers were motivated to attack the target as an animal industry, its state linkages further added to its appeal and alignment to the anarchist method of targeted attack.

Portland, Oregon—United States [2013]

In the US, recent anarchist direct actions in Portland have utilized ALF-style attacks yet quickly grew to adopt the internationalist anarchist moniker of the FAI. The first such incident in the spree occurred in June 2013 and involved activists gluing locks and destroying windows with glass etching solution. The communiqué, released to *Indymedia*, and signed "Anonymous

Anarchists" (2013), speaks of the "exploitat[ion] and killing' of marine animals" and encourages more attacks:

> For those in Portland in the business of ecological devastation and mass murder, get out or be forced out. To those who are inspired by our action, know that these actions can be carried out with ease and that the capitalists are incredibly vulnerable. (Anonymous Anarchists, 2013)

The short communiqué, penned under an anarchist moniker, advocates direct action for animal liberation to achieve these aims. Around 15 June 2013, activists announced that they had glued the locks of a business dealing in sheepskins and used their communiqué to express solidarity with "long-term anarchist prisoners" and those under harassment from grand juries (Anonymous, 2013e). The attacker(s) used their 59-word communiqué to twice show solidarity with specific anarchist reference points. A few weeks later, "Autonomist Animal Allies" used Portland *Indymedia* once again to announce that they had glued the locks of a slaughterhouse specializing in exotic meats. The attacker(s) speak directly to anarchists urging:

> With this action, we hope to awake a sleeping giant. This action is for those who plot and dream. This is for every anarchist who dreams of taking illegal action but has not yet. As the capitalists destroy everything beautiful in this world, and the vicious state engages in more torture and repression to protect them, we must continue to attack. (Autonomist Animal Allies, 2013)

The author(s) also posted home phone numbers for high-ranking staffers—noting the presence of company vehicles at their homes—providing future targets for attacks.

Approximately three weeks later, nearly the same name is used—this time *Anarchist* Animal Allies not *Autonomist* Animal Allies—to claim responsibility for the repeated gluing of locks of an exotic bird seller. Speaking to an anti-speciesist, anarchist politic, the author(s) state: "We will not stand complacent and let businesses like this one commodify animals and disrespect nature. We will do everything in our power to drive them into the ground" (Anarchist Animal Allies, 2013). As tribute towards the anarchist movement facing repression, the writer(s) states: "For the grand jury resisters. Your silence makes us collectively strong" (Anarchist Animal Allies, 2013). Around 9 August 2013 Portland's *Indymedia* is once again sent an anonymous, unsigned communiqué claiming responsibility for gluing the locks of a "steer market," stating, "Our crimes are in solidarity with the animals under the knife, and are inspired by all of the creative destruction taking place as of late by anarchists and animal liberationists in Portland. Keep it up, Portland!" (Anonymous, 2013g). Not only does the language of "creative destruction" speak to a larger political trend in insurrectionary anarchism, but the explicit acknowledgment of increased anarchist and ALF-styled activity in the Portland area speaks to activists' awareness of movement trends and anonymously-reported actions.

Later that same year, the influence of global insurrectionary struggle was once again made prominent by an attack claimed under the internationalist moniker of the FAI. In a brief communiqué issued around 16 September 2013, the "FAI–OREGON" (2013) claimed responsibility for slashing the tires of a dairy company's vans. The author(s) stated that they acted to "continue the momentum of direct action targeting speciesist companies in Portland ... We are happy to see the surge in illegal actions in Portland. Keep fighting. Until all humyn and non-humyn prisons are destroyed" (FAI-OREGON, 2013). This language speaks to not only the spree of incidents, but also a liberationist, anti-speciesist politic. By claiming the relatively minor act of property destruction with the FAI moniker, the attacker(s) communicate a strong message of solidarity and ideological affiliation with the larger network of dispersed globally.

Conclusion

The so-called insurrectionary turn in the anarchist politic of attack has fostered an increasingly-intersectional period of struggle. What marks this tendency as distinct is its break from previous social movement models; fighting for total liberation, without mediation or reformism whilst avoiding the leveraging of one social ill at the behest of downtrodden species. In the animal *rights* model popularized by PETA, the movement frequently campaigns for the lives of non-human animals through the exploitive treatment of race, class, sexuality and gender/sex expression (Ann, 2008; Deckha, 2008; Kelleher, 2009). In comparison, those who have taken to fight for all species through broken windows, burned McDonald's and exploding bombs have used the political space created by the post-attack communiqué to further a newly liberatory politic of resistance to domination that avoids identity and issue-based politics and instead seeks to destroy the mechanisms of oppression through confrontational direct action. These communiqués and other anonymously-authored texts present the borders of a newly invigorated anti-state, anti-capitalist framework that asserts, "no bosses, no masters, no speciesist hierarchies, through whatever means necessary."

More than five years have passes since this historical review was written, and in that time, anarchists have continued to fiercely strike against the State, capital, and for the liberation of all life. While the preceding discussion does not take into account how this past half decade has progressed, both the insurrectionary attack networks and more generalized animal liberation actions seem to have declined. To a degree, these energies have shifted in response to the rise of other, interlinked challenges such as the rise of white nationalism, anti-migrant xenophobia, and fights against pipelines. Social movements and patterns of attack have ways of cyclically waxing and waning and with the expansion of large infrastructure and extraction projects in so-called North America—such as the Dakota Access Pipeline and Mountain Valley Pipeline—the explicit focus on animal exploitation seems to have taken a temporary backset to other focuses. How these movements will proceed to grow and change into the future is anyone's guess.

References

Act for Freedom Now! (2011, December 3). *Athens: Antispeciesist protest against the fur and leather industry.* Retrieved from actforfree.nostate.net/?p=6800

ALF. (2013, July 21). *News July 21 2013.* Retrieved from www.directaction.info/news_july21_13.htm

ALF. // Chaotics. (2013, February 26). *News February 26 2013.* Retrieved from www.directaction.info/news_feb26_13.htm

ALF/ELF. (2013, October 28). *News October 28 2013.* Retrieved from http://www.directaction.info/news_oct28_13.htm

ALF/FAI-SEALS on Tour. (2013, July 23). *Two dolphins liberated from Yevpatoria dolphinarium by 'SEALS on tour' cell of the Animal Liberation Front – Informal Anarchist Federation (Ukraine).* Retrieved from 325.nostate.net/?p=8356

Anarchist Animal Allies. (2013, August 11). *News August 11b 2013.* Retrieved from http://www.directaction.info/news_aug11b_13.htm anarchists (2013, April 18). *Anarchists respond to police killing of dogs.* Retrieved from anarchistnews.org/content/anarchists-respond-police-killing-dogs

Angry Foxes Cell, & ACAB. (2013, August 29). *News August 29 2013.* Retrieved from http://www.directaction.info/news_aug29_13.htm

Animal Defense League. (2004, March 2). AR-News: re: (nyc) PARTY FOR RELEASED POLITICAL PRISONER [Listserve]. Retrieved October 19, 2012, from AR-News website: lists.envirolink.org/pipermail/ar-news/Week-of-Mon-20040301/020488.html

Ann. (2008, August 15). Same old shit from PETA. Retrieved August 12, 2019, from Feministing website: http://feministing.com/2008/08/15/same_old_tactic_from_peta_with/

Anonymous. (2002). *Call to Action: World Economic Forum ('wear_blac.txt').* Retrieved from nyc.indymedia.org/media/text/_wear_blac.txt

Anonymous. (2004, February 23). *[Break_The_Chains] CALLING ALL NORTHEAST ACTIVISTS!* Retrieved from http://groups.yahoo.com/neo/groups/cuaf/conversations/topics/4818?var=1

Anonymous. (2012a, October 6). *Fuck colonialist holidays.* Retrieved from anarchistnews.org/content/fuck-colonialist-holidays

Anonymous. (2012b, December 8). *Athens: Anarchist-antispeciesist demonstration was fiercely attacked by cops.* Retrieved from http://en.contrainfo.espiv.net/2012/12/08/athens-anarchist-antispeciesist-demonstration-was-fiercely-attacked-by-cops/

Anonymous. (2013a). *Anarchy–Civil or subversive? A collection of texts against civil Anarchism.* Retrieved from http://325.nostate.net/wp-content/uploads/2013/11/civil-anarchism-book.pdf

Anonymous. (2013b, January 2). *News January 2 2013.* Retrieved from http://www.directaction.info/news_jan02_13.htm

Anonymous. (2013c, January 6). *Vancouver, BC: Molotov attack on cap car claimed by ALF.* Retrieved from pugetsoundanarchists.org/content/vancouver-bc-molotov-attack-cop-car-claimed-alf

Anonymous. (2013d, January 11). *Bristol: Screws cars damaged (UK).* Retrieved from 325.nostate.net/?p=6867

Anonymous. (2013e, June 15). *News June 15 2013.* Retrieved from http://www.directaction.info/news_jun15_13.htm

Anonymous. (2013f, July 12). *News July 12 2013.* Retrieved from http://www.directaction.info/news_july12_13.htm

Anonymous. (2013g, August 9). *News August 9 2013.* Retrieved from http://www.directaction.info/news_aug09_13.htm

Anonymous. (2013h, October 11). *News October 11 2013.* Retrieved from http://www.directaction.info/news_oct11_13.htm

Anonymous. (2013i, October 22). *İstanbul: Painted slogans in Turkish and Greek on the walls of Şişli by anarchists.* Retrieved from http://en.contrainfo.espiv.net/2013/10/22/istanbul-painted-slogans-in-turkish-and-greek-on-the-walls-of-sisli-by-anarchists/

Anonymous. (2013j, November 14). Kiwi Mink oil contaminated in stores across United States. Retrieved January 31, 2014, from North American Animal Liberation Press Office website: https://animalliberationpressoffice.org/NAALPO/2013/11/14/2539/

Anonymous Anarchists. (2013, June). *News July 6 2013.* Retrieved from www.directaction.info/news_july06_13.htm

Anti-speciesists. (2012, August 16). *Responsibility claim for the attack on the Thessalic meat market, Volos Greece* (Act for Freedom Now! & bouburAs, Trans.). Retrieved from actforfree.nostate.net/?p=10970

Autonomist Animal Allies. (2013, July 8). *News July 8 2013.* Retrieved from http://www.directaction.info/news_july08_13.htm

Autonomous Cell "Silver bullets for police werewolves" of CCF RUSSIA. (2012, October 26). *Communique for the bombing of the police department in Ramenskoe (Russia)* (fromrussiawithlove.noblogs.org, Trans.). Retrieved from 325.nostate.net/?p=6514

Autonomous Fraction of Rebel Thieves FAI-FRI. (2012, May 7). *Bolivia: Claim for sabotage of Hipermaxi supermarkets in Cochabamba* (War on Society, Trans.). Retrieved from waronsociety.noblogs.org/?p=4502

Bash Back! (2010, March 3). *Bash Back!ers in support of autonomous animal action call for trans-species solidarity with Tillikum.* Retrieved from https://anarchistinternational. org/node/10815

CCF-Russia, & ELF-Russia. (2013, September 10). *News September 10 2013.* Retrieved from http://www.directaction.info/news_sep10_13.htm

Células Terroristas Por el Ataque Directo—Facción Anticivilizadora. (2011, September 5). Reivindicación de dos atentados realizados meses atras y aportes para el desarrollo de la praxis contra el sistema tecnológico industrial y la civilización. Retrieved January 31, 2014, from Liberación Total website: http://liberaciontotal.lahaine. org/?p=3653

Chicago Vegananarchist Wolf. (2013, July 2). *News July 2 2013.* Retrieved from www. directaction.info/news_july02_13.htm

CI-MSA/FAI-M. (2012, September 24). *Insurrectional Cell Mariano Sanchez Añon/ FAI claim responsibility for an armed attack against police (Mexico).* Retrieved from http://325.nostate.net/?p=6377

C.N.I. (Incendiary Nomad Cell). (2013, March 7). *News March 7 2013* (War on Society, Trans.). Retrieved from www.directaction.info/news_mar07_13.htm

DARTT. (2012, October 24). *Halloween "Trick or Treat" Demos: DARTT and Anarchist Alliance DC Network team up.* Retrieved from http://dc.indymedia.org/newswire/ display/153781/index.php

Deckha, M. (2008). Disturbing images: Peta and the feminist ethics of animal advocacy. *Ethics and the Environment, 13*(2), 35–76.

ELF/FAI–IRF. (2011, November 2). *Words of solidarity with conspiracy of cells of fire from some members of Russian Earth Liberation Front/FAI-IRF (Russia).* Retrieved from 325.nostate.net/?p=3405

FAI/IRF Nicola and Alfredo Cell. (2013, December 24). Greece: "Green Nemesis" project, sabotage against Coca-cola and Nestle products by FAI/IRF (24/12/2013). Retrieved January 31, 2014, from Inter Arma website: https://interarma.info/en/ 2013/12/25/sabotage_coca_cola_nestle/

FAI-OREGON. (2013, September 16). *News September 16 2013.* Retrieved from http:// directaction.info/news_sep16_13.htm

FLA Bolivia. (2011, November 6). *News November 6 2011* (Liberación Total, Trans.). Retrieved from http://www.directaction.info/news_nov06_11.htm

Heterogeneous Faction of Libertarian Weichafes [HFLW]. (2013, January 25). *News January 25 2013* (War on Society, Trans.). Retrieved from www.directaction.info/ news_jan25_13.htm

Immergut, K. J., Engdall, K. A., Peifer, S. F., & Ray, J. C. (2007, May 4). *Government's Sentencing Memorandum in the United States District Court for the District of Oregon [case numbers CR 06-60069-AA, CR 06-60070-AA, CR 06-60071-AA, CR 06-60078-AA, CR 06-60079-AA, CR 06-60080-AA, CR 06-60120-AA, 06-60122-AA,*

06-60123-AA, 06-60124-AA, 06-60125-AA, 06-60126-AA]. United States District Court for the District of Oregon.

Incendiary Nucleus of Action for the Spread of the Revolt/FAI-FRI. (2011, November 8). *News November 8 2011* (Liberación Total, Trans.). Retrieved from http://www.directaction.info/news_nov08b_11.htm

International FAI. (2011, September 13). *"Rain & Fire" – Statement from a UK FAI sector.* Retrieved from 325.nostate.net/?p=3032

ITS. (2011a, May 22). *Second communique from individualists tending toward the wild.* Retrieved from http://waronsociety.noblogs.org/?p=3093

ITS. (2011b, August 15). *Individualists tending toward the wild claim responsibility for package bomb that wounded two professors.* Retrieved from http://waronsociety.noblogs.org/?p=1523

ITS. (2011c, September 21). *Fourth communique from individualists tending toward the wild.* Retrieved from http://waronsociety.noblogs.org/?p=2913

ITS. (2012, January 29). *Sixth communique from individualists tending toward the wild.* Retrieved from http://waronsociety.noblogs.org/?p=3162

ITS. (2013, February 19). *Seventh communique from individualists tending toward the wild* (War on Society, Trans.). Retrieved from http://325.nostate.net/?p=7218

Kaczynski, T. J. (2010). *Technological slavery: The collected writings of Theodore J. Kaczynski, a.k.a. "The Unabomber."* Port Townsend, WA: Feral House.

Kelleher, K. (2009, January 28). PETA Disgusts Americans with adolescent advertising. Retrieved August 12, 2019, from Jezebel website: https://jezebel.com/peta-disgusts-americans-with-adolescent-advertising-5140840

Kropotkin, P. (1902). *Mutual aid: A factor of evolution* (Online). Retrieved from http://dwardmac.pitzer.edu/Anarchist_Archives/kropotkin/mutaidcontents.html

Loadenthal, M. (2011). Operation Splash Back!: Queering animal liberation through the contributions of neo-insurrectionist queers. *Journal of Critical Animal Studies, 10*(3), 85–112.

Marut, R. (2009, March 28). The SHAC model. Retrieved January 31, 2014, from *CrimethInc. Far East Blog* website: http://www.crimethinc.com/texts/rollingthunder/shac.php

Mauricio Morales Incendiary Brigade. (2013, January 14). *News January 14 2013* (War on Society, Trans.). Retrieved from www.directaction.info/news_jan14_13.htm

Ng, S., & Binkley, C. (2013, November 22). S.C. Johnson Pulls Kiwi Mink oil after animal rights threat. *Wall Street Journal.* Retrieved from http://online.wsj.com/news/articles/SB10001424052702303653004579214373428064280

North American Animal Liberation Press Office, & Sheen, N. (2013, August 24). [animallibpress] Summer E-Newsletter [Press Office]. Retrieved August 25, 2013, from North American Animal Liberation Press Office website: animalliberationpressoffice.org pfm. (2013, November 11). *Contemporary Israeli Anarchism: A History.* Retrieved from http://www.crimethinc.com/blog/2013/11/11/contemporary-israeli-anarchism-a-history/

Schurr, K. (2002, September 12). *News Article on Repression of the SHAC Campaign.* Retrieved from pets.groups.yahoo.com/group/HLSsucks/message/370

Some Wayward Nocturnals–FAI/IRF. (2012a, April 12). *Bolivia: Incendiary attack on Bank of the Andes ATM in La Paz* (War on Society, Trans.). Retrieved from waronsociety.noblogs.org/?p=4183

Some Wayward Nocturnals–FAI/IRF. (2012b, May 12). *News May 12 2012* (Liberación Total, Trans.). Retrieved from http://www.directaction.info/news_may12_12.htm

The Talon Conspiracy. (2013, October 17). Scott Crow and Josh Harper on anarchism and animal rights. Retrieved January 31, 2014, from The Talon Conspiracy website: http://thetalonconspiracy.com/2013/10/scott-crow-and-josh-harper-on-anarchism-and-animal-rights/

Two Sequoias, ALF-FAI. (2012, June 4). *Crematory used for incinerating bodies of stray dogs is bombed in Chernigov, Ukraine.* Retrieved from actforfree.nostate.net/?p=9822

Two Sequoias, ALF-FAI. (2013, March 8). *Krasnodar: 'Two Sequoias ALF-FAI' set horse free in the wild (Russia).* Retrieved from http://directaction.info/news_mar04_13.htm & 325.nostate.net/?p=7318

Wild Hogs, ALF-FAI. (2012, October 28). *Tver: "Wild Hogs, ALF-FAI" sabotage a hunt with various actions (Russia).* Retrieved from 325.nostate.net/?p=6523

Wolfpack, ELF/ALF-Russia, FAI. (2012, September 27). *News September 27b 2012.* Retrieved from www.directaction.info/news_sep27b_12.htm

Wolfpack, ELF/FAI. (2013, March 13). *News March 13b 2013.* Retrieved from www.directaction.info/news_mar13b_13.htm

Wrists of Fire Insurrectional Command, FAI–IRF. (2011, December 22). *Bolivia: Communiqué from the wrists of fire insurrectional command FAI-IRF.* Retrieved from http://waronsociety.noblogs.org/?p=2634

Contributors

Will Boisseau completed his Ph.D. at Loughborough University. His research focuses on the place of animal advocacy within the British left, particularly on the relationship between the anarchistic/direct action and legislative wings of the movement. Through this research he explores a range of concepts including speciesism, total liberation and intersectionality. He is also interested in locating a class analysis within Animal Studies. Will is a member of the Anarchism Research Group and his research interests include Anarchist Studies, Radical Animal Studies, labour History and Social Movement Studies.

Erika Cudworth is Professor of Feminist Animal Studies in the School of Social Sciences at the University of East London, UK, where she teaches Sociology and International Relations. Her books include *Social Lives with Other Animals: tales of sex, death and love* (2011) and *The Emancipatory Project of Posthumanism* (2017, with Stephen Hobden).

Michael Loadenthal is a researcher, trainer, and professor, and serves as a postdoctoral scholar at the University of Cincinnati, the Executive Director of the Peace and Justice Studies Association, and the founder and Executive Director of the Prosecution Project. His research focuses on political violence, social movements, and security through the lens of discourse, rhetoric, technology, and (anti)securitization. Dr. Loadenthal's publications have appeared in dozens of academic journals, books, and social movement publications. His first single-authored book, *The Politics of Attack* (2017) investigated contemporary, clandestine networks of insurrectionary anarchists and the development of the communique. Dr. Loadenthal has taught a variety of courses at Georgetown University, Miami University, George Mason University, the University of Cincinnati, the University of Malta, Jessup Correctional Institution, and the DC Jail. He holds a Ph.D. from the School for Conflict Analysis and Resolution (George Mason University) and a Master's Degree from the Centre for the Study of Terrorism and Political Violence (University of St Andrews).

Anthony J. Nocella II, Ph.D., scholar-activist, is an Assistant Professor in the Department of Criminal Justice and Criminology in the Institute of Public Safety at Salt Lake Community College. He is the editor of the Peace Studies Journal and Transformative Justice Journal, and co-editor of five book series including Critical Animal Studies and Theory with Lexington Books and Hip Hop Studies and Activism with Peter Lang Publishing. He has published over fifty book chapters or articles and over forty books, with many being translated in different languages. He has been interviewed by New York Times, Washington Post, Houston Chronicles, Fresno Bee, Fox, CBS, CNN, C-SPAN, and Los Angeles Times.

David Naguib Pellow, Ph.D., is the Dehlsen and Department Chair of Environmental Studies and Director of the Global Environmental Justice Project at the University of California, Santa Barbara where he teaches courses on environmental and social justice, race/class/gender and environmental conflict, human-animal conflicts, sustainability, and social change movements that confront our socioenvironmental crises and social inequality. He has volunteered for and served on the Boards of Directors of several community-based, national, and international organizations that are dedicated to improving the living and working environments for people of color, immigrants, indigenous peoples, and working class communities, including the Global Action Research Center, the Center for Urban Transformation, the Santa Clara Center for Occupational Safety and Health, Global Response, Greenpeace USA, and International Rivers.

Kyle Ramsey-Sumner is an activist-scholar whose primary research interests focus on the intersections of animal liberation, anarchism, and Christian theology through the lens of total liberation. He has a Master of Theological Studies degree from Iliff School of Theology where he explored and wrote on the failure of the field of animal theology to live up to its potential for liberation. Kyle is a member of Students for Critical Animal Studies. Along with his interests in Christian animal ethics and eco-theology, he is interested in mobilizing white, working class communities to fight racism in the rural south.

Piper Ramsey-Sumner lives outside of Tallahassee, Florida with her husband, Kyle. She aspires to create a pastoral approach to anti-racist community building in the rural south. Currently a Master of Divinity student at Iliff School of Theology, Piper's research explores chaplaincy for political activists, radical animal theology, anti-capitalist/anti-patriarchal ministry, and the implementation of process thought in pastoral care. Her present involvement with radical animal studies is grounded in her understanding of total liberation and a praxis-oriented political and spiritual lifestyle.

Kim Socha is author of *Animal Liberation and Atheism: Dismantling the Procrustean Bed* and is employed as a social emergency response worker for those facing family violence, housing instability, addiction, and mental health crises.

Richard J. White is a Reader in Human Geography. Greatly influenced by anarchism and anarchist geographies, his main research and teaching interests address a range of ethical and economic landscapes rooted in the context of social justice and total liberation movements. He recently co-edited the book *Anarchism and Animal Liberation: Essays on Complementary Elements of Total Liberation* (McFarland Press, 2015); and has written chapters for *Fighting Academic Repression and Neoliberal Education* (Peter Lang, 2017); *The Handbook of Neoliberalism* (Routledge, 2016), *Critical Animal Geographies* (Routledge, 2015), *Critical Animal Studies Approach to Animal Liberation An Introduction to an Intersectional Social Justice* (Peter Lang, 2014) and *The Accumulation of Freedom: Writings on Anarchist Economics* (AK Press, 2012).

Aaron Zellhoefer had been involved in many grassroots campaigns in the late 1990's and early 2000's. Aaron was involved in many fur campaigns and moved onto the campaign against Huntingdon Life Sciences, "Stop Huntingdon Animal Cruelty." After being involved in grassroots campaigning, Aaron got involved in politics. He worked to successfully prevent LGBT marriage from being banned, and then helped to get it passed into law. He also worked on several anti vivisection laws. Aaron is currently an ultramarathon runner. He lives in New York City with his husband Kevin, and their two beagles, Junior and Raymond.

Index

RADICAL ANIMAL STUDIES AND TOTAL LIBERATION

Anthony J. Nocella II, SERIES EDITOR

The **Radical Animal Studies and Total Liberation** book series branches out of Critical Animal Studies (a field co-founded by Anthony J. Nocella II) with the argument that criticism is not enough. Action must follow theory. This series demands that scholars are engaged with their subjects both theoretically and actively via radical, revolutionary, intersectional action for total liberation. Founded in anarchism, the series provides space for scholar-activists who challenge authoritarianism and oppression in their many daily forms. **Radical Animal Studies and Total Liberation** promotes accessible and inclusive scholarship that is based on personal narrative as well as traditional research, and is especially interested in the advancement of interwoven voices and perspectives from multiple radical, revolutionary social justice groups and movements such as Black Lives Matter, Idle No More, Earth First!, the Zapatistas, ADAPT, prison abolition, LGBTTQQIA rights, disability liberation, Earth Liberation Front, Animal Liberation Front, political prisoners, radical transnational feminism, environmental justice, food justice, youth justice, and Hip Hop activism.

To order other books in this series please contact our Customer Service Department:

PETERLANG@PRESSWAREHOUSE.COM (WITHIN THE U.S.)

ORDERS@PETERLANG.COM (OUTSIDE THE U.S.)

To find out more about the series or browse a full list of titles, please visit our website:

WWW.PETERLANG.COM